A Porch Sofa Almanac

A Porch Sofa Almanac

Peter Smith

University of Minnesota Press
Minneapolis
London

Published by the University of Minnesota Press
111 Third Avenue South, Suite 290
Minneapolis, MN 55401-2520
http://www.upress.umn.edu

Library of Congress Cataloging-in-Publication Data
Smith, Peter
    A porch sofa almanac / Peter Smith.
        p.   cm.
ISBN 978-0-8166-7232-5 (pb : alk. paper)
    1. Minnesota—Anecdotes. I. Title.
    F606.6.S65 2010
    977.6—dc22
                        2010013982

Printed in the United States of America on acid-free paper

The University of Minnesota is an equal-opportunity educator and employer.

16 15 14 13 12 11 10   10 9 8 7 6 5 4 3 2

Contents

Preface

THIS IS A BOOK of short essays about small things. Most of them aired as commentaries on Minnesota Public Radio's *Morning Edition* with Cathy Wurzer. There's this window in programming on weekday mornings around ten to seven when there is room for Minnesota news, weather, and what-have-you. Each of these essays was a Tuesday morning what-have-you.

My assignment from MPR was simple and mercifully vague: try to do something about Minnesota. Okay, I thought. Can do. Minnesota is full of people, places, and whatnot that fill the bill perfectly.

Some days, as I observe Minnesota and write these pieces, it's as if we are all at a wedding reception in one of those old-time ballrooms, with friends mingling, kids tearing around, and the old people sitting there, looking on. It's like standing around, holding a long-neck beer and talking with old friends. Other days, it's like wandering through a flea market: I rummage around, pick stuff up, and show you. Minnesota has plenty to rummage through.

For example, my elderly mother-in-law has begun to play fast and loose with freshness codes when she cooks. They didn't have freshness codes on the farm back when she was growing up, and she for darn sure doesn't need any freshness codes now. Or consider the persistent, low-grade, societal tug—that nagging peer pressure Minnesotans feel. We all live with the unshakable idea that across the street the neighbors are peeking from behind the blinds, telepathically urging us to weed the dandelions, paint the trim, mow the lawn.

The same tug tells us other drivers want and expect us to merge for an exit miles before we need to. We feel them willing us into the back of the line of cars waiting to exit even as other traffic moves freely; we feel them resent us when we don't. The tug makes us wait patiently at stoplights while the driver ahead of us shakes off his daydream and realizes the light has turned green. In fast food joints, it helps us wait while the customer ahead of us (who had plenty of time to study the menu while he stood in line) struggles to make up his mind and order. After all, Minnesota gave birth to Burger King, the hamburger chain where you get to stand in line twice: once to order, once again to pick up your food.

Often, these short essays about small things are about change of some sort. The fault line between who we were and who we are becoming runs the length of the state and coughs up stuff to write about in the same way that seismic fault lines cough up diamonds. There is an antique store in Crosby with several shelves full of old Hudson's

Bay blankets—moth-eaten things, seventy, eighty, and ninety years old, all graying and fading and neatly folded, waiting for someone to come along and buy them again. The blankets outlasted the couples they used to keep warm. What with global warming, they may well have outlasted the kinds of winters they were designed for in the first place. Standing there, looking at those lonely old blankets, you can almost see the bedrooms they came from. The wood floors. The rag rugs. The Sears, Roebuck bed and dresser sets, the veneer on the dresser lifting, peeling back where she spilled nail polish remover in 1952. The open window. A loon calling in the night. An old-fashioned alarm clock ticking close by.

In Minnesota, you see stuff to write about every-where. You start to archive it.

Driving west from the Twin Cities, passing through small towns and county seats, you see those old six- and eight-unit motels, the small, family-owned ones. The kind where your grandfather, a furniture salesman who drove a maroon four-door Ford, used to stay. The signs out front used to advertise "Free Color TV!" or "Air Conditioning!" or "Phone In Every Room!" Except for the first night of his honeymoon, your grandfather never associated exclamation marks with lodging—and that honeymoon had been at the swank (by his standards) Curtis Hotel in downtown Minneapolis, not out here next to a freshly manured cornfield west of Cokato.

The small-town family motels are mostly empty now. The "Vacancy" signs are always on unless there's a big wedding or family reunion in town. Grass grows through the cracks in the blacktop out front. Inside, the knotty pine paneling smells of cigarette smoke and mildew. Ghosts of long-dead traveling salesmen sit in their boxer shorts on threadbare chenille spreads, writing up orders from some big day long ago, their suit trousers hanging neatly on those hangers you can't take off the rack behind the front door.

You drive past. You sense the old salesmen in there. You make a note. Someday, you will come back in a maroon four-door Ford. You'll check in, sit down on the bed, and write something about them.

If not the motels of small-town Minnesota, then maybe the ice fishing shacks of Mille Lacs. They stand there in the weeds by the road all summer, rank upon rank of them, some homemade, some factory built, eyesores all. But if you have ever been out there on the ice at night, under the stars in the quiet and big cold of January, you won't hold this spate of summer-ugly against them.

If nothing else changes, there are always the miniseasons through which Minnesota slides. No two days, weeks, or months are exactly alike. You keep your eyes open. You make a few notes.

We organized these pieces like a slightly off-kilter almanac. They start at the point where September kicks over from late summer to fall—when, all but overnight, the sumac goes red, the maples go red-orange, the birch and popples go yellow, and you want to go back to school no matter how old you are. Somewhere across the lake somebody is working a chainsaw—a tool worthy of a short essay itself. The air is cool and warm at the same time, and the world feels damn good. October arrives, with firewood to split and old familiar books to reread. November comes sulking in, cloudy and gray, blustery as a brother-in-law bent on arguing postelection politics at Thanksgiving dinner. December—the holidays, darkness, brooding. New Year's, ice fishing, cabin fever, this and that. All the way through the year back to September, always trying to say something about Minnesota. We could have started at the beginning of the calendar year, but this feels more Minnesotan somehow.

Thank you to Minnesota Public Radio; to Chris Worthington, Cathy Wurzer, the always acerbic Jim Bickal, Curtis Gilbert, Julie Siple, and Gary Eichten. Thank you to Sid Farrar, John Schaubach, and Sonny Clark. Most of all, thank you to Miss Minnie Nelson of Fridley, Minnesota, who, on a brilliant, blue Minnesota October day long ago, dropped by my place to wash her car.

Porch Sofas

THE MINNEAPOLIS CITY COUNCIL wants to ban porch sofas. They say they look trashy. They get moldy and attract mice and other rodents. They catch fire.

The grumpy suburban guy in me says, "Darn right. Get 'em out of here. Enough is enough." But the hippie in me remembers porch sofas past. The concave cushions, the perpetual sag. Warm evenings sitting out front, sipping long-neck beers, listening to music, watching traffic, and basking in the disapprobation of older neighbors. Those were the days. It was flaming youth, not flaming sofas. Just who is the Minneapolis City Council to deny today's young people the innocent pleasure of a porch sofa?

Old sofas and young adulthood were made for each other. Except for a car, a used sofa was the biggest thing you owned in your twenties. Whether you inherited it from an aunt, acquired it when you broke up with your roommates, retrieved it from your parents' basement, or found it on the street wearing a sign that said "Free," it was yours. And it was with you for quite a while.

Your mother hated it. Company slept on it. It outlasted at least two meaningful relationships. You moved it three or four times, and if you lived in certain parts of Nordeast or in some sections of south Minneapolis or Dinkytown or some other college neighborhood, it eventually wound up on a porch.

Did that make you trashy? No. It just made you young. And relatively poor. And happy.

Then one enchanted evening, somebody dropped by and shared your sofa and your beer and your music. One thing led to another, and before you knew exactly what you'd gotten yourself into, you were married. Your porch sofa was gone, replaced by a new, Scotchgarded living room model, end tables, a coffee table, and matching lamps.

Just as well. You had a new home, mortgage payments and all, in a neighborhood that didn't approve of porch sofas. You settled in. You had kids. You raised them. You forgot.

Now the Minneapolis City Council wants to ban porch sofas.

In Ecclesiastes it says there's a time to every purpose under heaven. Well, this is no time for Minneapolis to ban porch sofas. Edina, sure. Eden Prairie, of course. But if Minneapolis—and I'll throw Saint Paul in there too—bans porch sofas, our young people will lose something more timeless than trashy. And you can drag me to the curb and slap a sign on me that says "Free."

Off to College:
A Parental Spreadsheet

THIS FALL, we're sending two of our young people off to college. Two—count 'em, two—one male, one female. While we are sorry to see them grow up and leave the nest, I've run a spreadsheet that we'll use to console ourselves when necessary.

For example, my spreadsheet and I are projecting a 40 percent reduction in clean towel consumption—maybe even a bit more in that my daughter the Swedish Norwegian Irish Princess is given to wearing bath towels as turbans until she fires up the hair dryer.

Speaking of the hair dryer, I expect a 100 percent decrease in the incidence of a plugged-in hair dryer sitting atop the toilet tank, a pet peeve of mine in that it compounds the difficulty of complying with my male-oriented toilet seat duties.

What else? Hmmm . . . let's see . . . a 100 percent reduction in returning empty orange juice containers to the fridge, a 50 to 80 percent reduction in the size of the shoe pile inside the front door, laundry loads off at least

50 percent. The incidence of dirty socks on the living room floor drops to near zero. Hair in the shower drain, near zero too.

The grocery bill gets slashed dramatically—almost enough to fund retirement, in fact. Car availability goes way up. So do the odds that the gas gauge will be above one-eighth of a tank.

The outflow of cash through the leak in my wallet should abate significantly, and the denomination on the bills going out will be smaller. (The college duo expects twenties. I can still buy off the grade-school kid with a five.)

I am projecting that the medicine chest will be 80 percent less cluttered. I am expecting a drastic reduction in shared toiletries, including deodorant and disposable razors, and a corresponding reduction in shared clothing items. My dress shirts were my son's dress shirts. Let's not mention boxer shorts. The spreadsheet goes on and on, and things look good. From the lint trap in the dryer to credit card balances in cyberspace, things look darned good.

Good-bye, my children. Go out there and do well. You can't see it on this spreadsheet, but by my calculations, your mother, your remaining sibling, and I will miss you at least 80 percent more than last semester.

School Starts This Morning

SCHOOL STARTS IN CITIES AND TOWNS all over Minnesota this morning. Even as I speak, tens of thousands of Minnesota households are roiling in first-morning-of-school chaos.

Adolescent siblings, who at this time yesterday had four more hours to sleep, are up. And surly. And fighting with one another for bathroom time. Hair dryers are whining. Radios are blaring. Curling irons are warming up on bathroom counters. You can almost feel the power grid sag under a demand for electricity that wasn't there this time yesterday.

Mothers, those queens of multitasking, are racing to get breakfasts on tables and lunches into brown paper bags even as they remind their elementary school kids who their teachers are, where their classrooms are, and who will or will not be there this afternoon when they get home from school.

As I speak, hundreds, if not thousands, of junior high kids are reciting their new locker assignments and lock combinations to themselves or writing them on the palms of their hands. They don't want to forget them and look uncool in the hall before class. Suddenly aware there are girls in the world, twelve-year-old boys, who only last spring would climb out of bed and into whatever clothes lay on the floor, are anguishing over which new shirt to wear and how to part their hair. Some may even be brushing their teeth without being told.

Across the state right now thousands of family dogs and cats are looking on. They're aware something is up and yet oddly at ease. They know all this doesn't pertain to them. They sense they can relax. This isn't a trip to the vet.

All those clocks on all those kitchen walls are moving inexorably forward. All those buses are on the way. Enjoy it while you can, Minnesota. Savor the chaos of this noisy, first morning of school because in a few minutes, there will be that last flurry—that grabbing of lunches and book bags and that dash for the door. Then the first-morning-of-school chaos will be over for another year and, house to themselves, a little sadder for the solitude, Minnesota's cats and dogs will adjourn to the patch of morning sunlight on the living room floor to doze in contented, never-to-be-educated tranquility. All day long.

We Want to Go Back, Too

THE FRESHMAN CLASS has moved into the dorms. They've been oriented and now the upper classes are back on campus, too. The leaves on the trees along the mall have begun to change. The college community is settling in for another year. And somewhere down deep, part of me still thinks I ought to be heading back to school, too.

It's been decades, but every fall I get that old tug. I want to go back to my real school with my real class-mates—like we were back then, not the middle-aged alumni we've become. I've held up remarkably well, but I don't like what time has done to my classmates—making them all gray and wrinkly and stodgy and responsible.

It all happened so fast. One minute you're borrow-ing a guy's fake ID to go buy beer, and the next you're at some alumni function, holding a plastic glass of Chablis while he stands there, sprouting eyebrows and ear hair and giving you stock tips. Or that girl shows up, the one you met at the freshman mixer and were supposed to marry. You were an item for a while there, but something happened and you went your separate ways. Now she's over there, across the room, looking a little matronly, carrying her purse like Queen Elizabeth. And lord knows, you're no Adonis yourself anymore. So you toss off your Chablis, set the glass down, and sidle toward the door.

It's that old college continuum. You climb on the day you set foot on campus, and you never ever get off. You and the rest of your class just slide down the class notes in the alumni magazine—from wedding and birth announcements to career and business blurbs to retirements and lifetime achievement awards and big donations to the general fund to—well, we all know where it ends, don't we?

Still, it's fall. The kids are all back at school. That tug is there in your heart. Sure, you've got work, family, a life to live, all those obligations. Yet down deep you always kind of wonder—who are they playing at the football game on Saturday?

In Praise of Small-Town Football

IT'S HARD TO FIND good small-town high school football these days. Proper football, played by a mismatched
set of local boys—some tall and skinny, some average
size, some short, some extra wide, all wearing patched
uniforms and battered helmets that went out of style ten
years ago, all out to defend their town's honor from those
no-goodniks from thirty miles down the road.

It's hard to find those out-of-tune marching bands
hammering away at "Jeremiah Was a Bullfrog," the horn
section coming in two-thirds of a beat after the drums.
And those out-of-shape middle-aged refs who teach
high school English two counties over and promised
The Wife this would be the last season they would ref?
Well, The Wife must have prevailed, because they're
hard to find, too.

These days the big suburban schools don't have football teams; they have programs. They don't have fields;
they have complexes with aluminum bleachers two stories high and training facilities to rival the Vikings' Eden
Prairie headquarters. The school district's lawyers suited

up to oversee the design of these places. Everything is fenced off with eight-foot chain link to keep fans from the players—and from visiting fans.

Meanwhile, outstate, an old geezer can still grab a cup of refreshment stand coffee and lean on the old snow fence at the back of the end zone and BS with other old geezers about the '56 team. Or the '66 team or '76 or '86. Wherever your inner geezer kicks in.

Small-town high school football is a nonhomogenized game full of quirky calls, eccentric scoreboard clocks, and delightful surprises. I was in a small town grocery store up north on a Friday night years ago when a local guy rushed in. They had blown a big fuse over at the football game. The lights were out. Did anybody know where he could find a replacement?

Want to bet the hometown boys were behind? That the game was suspended? That the blown fuse recovered miraculously and worked just fine the following week?

The Gophers and the Vikings put on a great show, but let's remember to celebrate small-town high school ball. Grab a cup of coffee. I'll see you somewhere along the snow fence.

Conflicted

I BIKE. I DRIVE. I am so conflicted. Touring the city on my bicycle, I loathe motorists who won't yield at crossings and stop signs or who turn in front of me and force me to hit the brakes. They have no sense of the effort it takes to establish and sustain momentum on a bicycle. Behind the wheel, I see bicyclists as selfish, "me first," road-hogging, stop sign–blowing boors. Especially the ones in spandex.

Whichever mode of transportation I happen to be using, I detest the other. I am my own road rage. One of these days, I'm going to cut myself off in traffic. It's going to come to blows, and when it does, boy howdy.

You would think that someone who bikes and drives would be able to resolve this natural conflict, that being able to roll a mile on the other guy's tires would help me find a balance somehow. Nope. I have no compassion for bikers when I drive. I have no empathy for motorists when I bike. If I encountered me at a four-way stop, I would almost certainly flip myself off.

On my bike, I try to give motorists who yield a

friendly little thank-you wave. But every time I do it, my inner motorist calls me a dork. Conversely, when an unyielding biker makes me stop the car short, I seethe, even though my inner biker reminds me I do this to motorists all the time. "Sure you do," says my inner motorist, "because you're a dork."

Luckily, winter is just around the corner. Another month or so and I'll retire the bike to the basement. I'll put it on one of those stationary stands in front of the TV, pedal away an hour or so a day, and keep my hostility skills sharp by seething at the political pundits until spring.

Autumn Golf

Aw, SHOOT. Fallen leaves on the fairway. The end of another season of golf.

Leaves on the fairway hide the ball and turn even a perfect drive into a problem. A shot that would have been a delight in June becomes an autumn nightmare as you mill around, brushing leaves aside with a fairway wood, searching, endlessly searching for that Top Flite 4 that's right around here somewhere.

Even if you do find your ball, two hundred yards up the fairway you repeat the process, searching anew in more leaves. And that gin-clear, yellow-tinted autumn light works against you. Something about it messes with your depth perception, making you hit the ball fat. Or thin. Or something other than perfect. No fair.

This time of year, you need perfect shots the way a squirrel needs acorns. You've got to store them up. It's going to be a long winter. You'll need the memory of a perfect nine iron to a sun-dappled green to warm your heart some cold February night. But the leaves on the fairway and the beautiful autumn light are working against you. Even that simple nine iron can jump up and bite you this time of year.

The cottonwood leaves are the saddest. There are so many of them. They are so trashy and brittle and yellow, and they lie out there, across the fairway, in a band maybe twenty-five yards wide right where your ball is going to land.

The course is autumn quiet—although there might be a crew of guys taking down a dead tree way out on the back nine, a tree they waited all summer to get to, not wanting to disrupt play when the course was busy. The sound of their chain saws and chipper is so sad somehow.

Other than the grounds crew, the course is empty. The people who played in leagues all summer are gone. We're down to the few, the proud, the golf addicts—mostly guys, and mostly playing solitaire, wandering around kicking at the leaves looking for a ball.

In a matter of weeks now, the newspapers will be full of ads for golf travel packages—three days, three rounds, hotel included, in some godforsaken place like Orlando or Las Vegas. That's tourist golf, not real golf. It's as plastic and phony as a Disney World parade.

The real golf will be back here, dormant under the snow, waiting for spring to creep up out of Iowa. Then those first few real golfers of the year will punch their tees through the frost in the ground, and the game that we lost under the autumn leaves in the fairway will begin all over again.

An Open Letter to
the City of Hopkins

City of Hopkins
1010 First Street South
Hopkins, MN 55343

Dear City of Hopkins:

This is to inform you that once again this year silver maple trees all over the neighborhood are refusing to comply with your leaf pickup ordinance and schedule. Once again, they are holding onto their leaves and stubbornly refusing to let go until after your leaf pick-up crews and trucks have passed through.

I suspect a plot. I suspect, too, that the plot is spreading. Keep your eye on the willows. They're hanging back and exhibiting signs of reluctance. And the elms. And the oaks. Even the oldest and stateliest towering trees—trees that have been solid citizens of Hopkins for eighty years or more—look as if, for whatever reason, they may choose to join the conspiracy this year.

The irony, of course, is that lowlife, riffraff trees like the cottonwoods and box elders, hanging out in the alleys and buckling garage foundations, have already done their part to comply with the ordinance. Their leaves are falling. And the decorative landscape trees, the crab apples and river birch clumps and the mountain ash, look like they will drop their leaves in time for homeowners to rake them, tarp them to the street, and meet your schedule, too.

It's the damned silver maples. They are the heart of the problem. They stand there, with their roots in the sewer lines and their leaves still green and firmly attached overhead, all smug. They stand there and scoff at the City of Hopkins ordinance.

It might be different if their leaves turned some dazzling color when they finally decided to go. A bright red or a blazing orange that extended the more beautiful aspects of fall into November. If silver maples did that, maybe we could forgive them for copping this attitude. But they don't. Malevolent spirits that they are, they turn their leaves an anemic yellow-green. They wait until they hear your trucks and street sweepers leave, then they drop them. Standing in the living room, looking out the picture window, you can almost hear a sarcastic "oops" as they let their leaves go.

Ten minutes later, it begins to snow. Five months after that, the last snows melt, and there are the silver maple leaves, still yellow-green and now moldy, limp as three-week-old lettuce in the refrigerator drawer and ready to blotch out the entire lawn until June.

Obviously, something has to be done, City of Hopkins. I say update the ordinance, or oil up the chain saws. It's time to drum some respect into those no-good silver maples. Time to take a stand and show them who is in charge.

The time is now. If we don't draw a line in the lawn, here and now, then pretty soon Hopkins will be just like St. Louis Park.

Signed,

An Irate Citizen

Hudson's Bay Blankets

LIKE A SWALLOW RETURNING to San Juan Capistrano in the spring, our Hudson's Bay blanket has returned to the foot of the bed for the winter. It's there now, folded back on itself, ready to be pressed into service on cool autumn nights.

Hudson's Bay blankets are the white wool ones with red, yellow, blue-black, and green stripes. They were first brought to the region by French Canadian voyageurs. But early Minnesotans knew a good, thick, scratchy blanket when they saw one, and a love affair that would last for centuries began.

Now, with fall well under way, Hudson's Bay blankets are reappearing all over the state, emerging from cedar chests and descending from closet shelves. Some of them smell vaguely of mothballs. All of them remind us who we really are, reassuring us that this much at least is still right with the world.

To a real Minnesotan, there is no greater pleasure than pulling a Hudson's Bay blanket up to your chin and sleeping these first really cool autumn nights away.

It restores your inner Minnesotan, like being baptized in the waters of Lake Superior, only it's warm.

While design and lifestyle magazines feature cabins and lake homes full of bedspreads, duvet covers, and quilts these days, that's not Minnesotan. Give us a Hudson's Bay blanket every time. That white background and those colorful stripes turn any bedroom into a still life worthy of one of the Wyeths.

Accept no substitutes. Spare yourself those thin, shrink-prone, olive drab surplus store numbers or those far-too-soft synthetic blankets that have shown up in discount store bedding departments lately. A real Hudson's Bay blanket is a Minnesota heirloom. On the bed as a spare blanket or on the sofa as an afghan, it all but becomes a member of the family.

The fall colors will peak in another couple of weeks. Then one night we'll hear the wind pick up and a cold rain start to fall, and the next morning those of us who get up early will look out and see that the trees are bare. Winter will be on the doorstep. Waiting for the coffee to perk, the early risers will slump just a bit.

Meanwhile, upstairs, safe, secure, ready for winter, those of us with Hudson's Bay blankets will pull them up to our chins, roll over, and grab fifteen more minutes of wonderful Minnesota autumn sleep.

Splitting Wood

It's autumn in Minnesota. It's time to go split some firewood. The air is warm enough to work in your shirtsleeves, yet cool enough to fend off a heavy sweat. This Indian summer weather is perfect for the job. And the tool for the job—a splitting maul—resonates wonderfully somewhere deep in your soul. Your great-great-great-grandfather mastered it. Those are his genes working in you.

There's an old Estonian proverb that says, "The work will teach you how to do it." Splitting firewood is like that. It teaches you how.

Years ago, you might have tried to power your way through every log on every swing. Now, the work has taught you patience and a certain stolidity. You've learned to look for the point where you can split the log with a lighter, perfectly placed swing. You've learned to work through knots and to point any fork in a log toward the dirt so the maul goes with the flow of the grain, not against it.

You've learned, too, that different kinds of wood split differently. Pulp woods like popple and birch give way easily. So does cedar. Ash, maple, and oak can be a little more obstinate. As for elm, forget about it. The grain runs every which way. Elm is all but impossible to split.

Different woods burn differently. Cedar makes great kindling. Birch and popple burn brighter, but much more quickly than hardwoods. Ash has some staying power, as does maple, but they don't burn quite as prettily as those lighter woods do. The longest burning of all is oak. It's perfect for heating with wood in the deep cold of January. But oak broods as it burns, as if it were sulking or giving up spirits. Who knows? Maybe it is.

A friend of mine up north has some five-thousand-year-old Indian mounds in his wood lot. We cleared three red oaks off them a few years back. When I'm up there in winter and see a stubborn, dark little fire in his living room wood burner, I ask him if it's Indian mound oak.

He nods. Yep, Indian mound oak.

We live in remarkable times. We've got the whole computerized, digitized world at our fingertips, and if that's not enough, we've got satellite radio and cable TV. But it's fall in Minnesota. If you don't mind, I'll just be out back enjoying the colors and the quiet and splitting wood.

The Menu Changes

DON'T LOOK NOW, but another of those annual Minnesota wonders is taking place. It's not the migrating birds, the fall colors, or the harvesting of the crops. The wonder I'm talking about is the changing of the supper menu.

From one end of the state to the other, Minnesotans have taken the annual turn away from lighter summer fare back toward that more substantial ballast we can't seem to resist once the temperature drops into the fifties and sunset starts arriving earlier.

So long, salad; hello, hotdish. We're talking dinner-at-the-kitchen-table food. Spaghetti with seared ground beef and canned mushrooms in watery tomato sauce. Meat loaf with brown gravy and mashed potatoes and real white bread and butter. Tuna-noodle and mushroom-soup hotdish. Food so bland and patently Minnesotan the entire family reaches for the pepper shaker at the same time.

These are recipes Grandma got from a neighbor, who found them in old issues of *Redbook* and *Ladies Home Journal*. Recipes so Minnesota traditional you could find all the ingredients in a Red Owl store—assuming you could find a Red Owl store.

In the old days, back on the farm, people worked meals like this off. There were crops to harvest, livestock to tend, and work to do. These days, every forkful translates into time on the treadmill. If you hop on right after supper and set the machine for eight miles an hour, you should be able to work it all off by bedtime.

Luckily, for those without access to treadmills, the annual change of menu syncs up nicely with the annual change of wardrobe. Nothing obscures a few extra winter menu pounds at an autumn neighborhood get-together quite like a bulky sweater or a lumberjack shirt worn tails out.

So tonight, when the family sits down to a big pan of that Nordic lasagna we all make (the lasagna with ground beef, canned tomatoes, and two pints of ricotta cheese), join hands, bow your heads, and say grace—or a prayer of resignation.

We are Minnesotans. This is what we eat in winter—let's accept it for what it is. Pass the pepper.

Good Autumn Reads

EVERY AUTUMN ABOUT THIS TIME, I find myself pulling a certain type of book off the shelf—nature essays by guys like Sigurd Olson and Aldo Leopold, guys who looked like they belonged in a Mark Trail comic strip, guys just made to wear heavy wool shirts and smoke pipes as they stared out cabin windows and wrote about migrating birds and the sound of the wind in the tall pine on the point above the lake.

There's something fundamentally positive and reassuring in their stuff. A steady, calm, grandfatherly tone that still works in an age when their grandchildren have become grandparents themselves. They are the perfect antidote, if only for an hour or two, to our globally warmed twenty-first-century angst and nihilism.

Even the artwork—woodcuts and pen-and-ink drawings of Boundary Waters lakes and birch trees and fence posts and upland birds and animal tracks—is reassuring. I'd chuck it all—the Internet, the Blackberry, cable television, everything—just to step into one of those drawings and take a nice long autumn walk with the author.

Leopold worked out of the hardscrabble Wisconsin River bottoms down around Baraboo. Olson preferred Ely, in Minnesota's canoe country. They both wrote in a style that's equal parts old *Field and Stream* magazine and Civilian Conservation Corps with maybe just a hint of Robert Frost. Coming of age when they did (almost exactly halfway back to the Victorians) and coming from the upper Midwest, they might have adopted a more florid style. They didn't, thank God. It's a subjective call, but I'd say Leopold and Olson's style is holding up a lot better than that of a contemporary of theirs—some guy named Hemingway.

Take a book by either one and open it anywhere. Indulge to your heart's content or bedtime, whichever comes first. You've found the perfect October evening read for here in the upper Midwest—or for anywhere. And October is such a special month.

"I love October," my son told me the other morning on the way to the bus stop. "It smells like pumpkins."

I can't wait to introduce him to Misters Leopold and Olson.

Darn Packers Fans

THE BIG GAME IS OVER. The Packers fans have gone back to Wisconsin. They were last seen on Interstate 94 early this morning, heading east up the hill on the far side of the St. Croix, taking their cheese heads and green and gold jerseys with them, trailing beer and brat fumes. Listen closely and you can still hear the last, fading strains of their polka music.

Say what you will about our neighbors to the east, they sure know how to have fun at a football game—win or lose. I don't know about you, but I'm jealous. Why can't we take as much simple-minded pleasure from our team as they do from theirs?

The answer is that we're thinking fans. If the unexamined life is not worth living, then the unexamined football team is not worth rooting for. So we overexamine and overanalyze absolutely everything about the Vikings: play selection, defense schemes, clock management, special teams—everything.

To compound the problem, the Vikings are a thinking team. For nearly fifty years they've tried to scheme their way to the championship—to outsmart the rest of the league the way Wile E. Coyote tries to outsmart the Road Runner. So far, no championships. The Vikes might as well send away for the *Acme Professional Football Playbook.*

The Buddha says that all unhappiness comes from wanting things too much. Maybe we thinking fans want to win too much. Over in Wisconsin, they're happy whether the Pack wins or loses. They don't care whether they're in first place. The only things they seem to want too much of are more beer and another brat. Darn Packers fans. Don't they know we won't be happy until they're unhappy? As unhappy as we are?

One border battle down, one to go. In a few weeks the Vikes will travel to Lambeau Field to take on the Pack. We have nearly a whole month to think up a scheme that will beat the Pack and turn their way-too-happy fans into scheming, thinking, unhappy fans just like us. We'll spend our time thinking; they'll spend theirs celebrating Octoberfest. We got them for sure this time.

Election Night Radio

OUR HOUSE was built in 1931, and a few years ago, a woman who grew up here in the 1940s came back to see how the place was holding up. She showed us the spot in the corner of the living room where the radio stood, and for some reason I've had an election night affinity for building a fire in the fireplace and listening to the returns on the radio rather than watching them on TV ever since.

Election results just feel better over the radio and in firelight. They're more momentous somehow—more important, more historic. Sitting in this room, leaning toward the radio, prodding the fire with the poker, it's easy to hear staticky echoes from other election nights, echoes with names like Hoover, Roosevelt, Truman, and Dewey. It's easier, too, to keep things in a larger perspective and parse the real meaning of events when you're staring into a sturdy little fire instead of staring at a screen full of people playing with large, computerized video maps and talking over one another.

As for the election night fire itself, I've split up and cached some special white oak. It came from a huge old tree that used to stand in our backyard. I counted the rings when the tree came down. It dated from the Grant administration, more than halfway back to George Washington. You can't get more American than that.

The radio is a modern twenty-dollar job—no match for the huge speaker and glowing dial of a 1940s-era superheterodyne parlor model. Still, it's a radio, and the room and the house and election night were made for it. Some years, it feels as if the spirits of great politicians from the past dropped in to sit down to listen to the returns with me.

No doubt the room has heard other big radio broadcasts—Fireside Chats from FDR, Joe Louis knocking out Max Schmelling, Edward R. Murrow reporting from London during the Blitz, and news of Pearl Harbor. But it's election night—history in the present tense—that makes for great living room radio.

When the last results are in and the losers and winners have made their speeches, I turn off the radio, bank the fire, step outside, look up at the stars, and smell the wood smoke on the November air. I think of the generations of Minnesotans who've listened to election night reports on the living room radio. To heck with the Internet and TV and all those new media. I hope election night living room radio is there for generations of Minnesotans yet to come.

No-Bleeping-Vember

THERE ARE CERTAIN MONTHS in Minnesota that, like certain members of every family, are cold, homely, and (let's admit it) just plain hard to love. November, for example. It's a succession of thirty days, each one shorter, colder, and grayer than the day before.

In November, overburdened teachers and librarians try to cheer us up by decorating bulletin boards with brown, yellow, orange, and black construction paper leaves and acorns and turkeys and pilgrim hats. While the rest of us are grateful for the effort, we don't really buy it. We're too glum. It's November, for crying out loud.

In November, the maintenance people at work come up from the basement where they have the boilers going full tilt, superheating us into a lassitude and ennui worthy of the dog days of summer. It's eighty degrees in the room. We're wearing turtlenecks. Looking at us as if we were cattle, they hold muted conferences with the office manager who called them. Then they open the plastic boxes they've put over the thermostats to save us from ourselves, and they reluctantly—the more sensitive among us would say resentfully—back the heat off a couple degrees.

Stupid building. Stupid boilers. Stupid month. Stupid workforce. Don't we know there's a cold front coming in from Bismarck? Don't we realize they'll just have to come back and dial the heat up again tomorrow? Shaking their heads, they return to the basement and resume doing whatever it is maintenance people do in the basement in November.

In November in Minnesota, nature colludes against us. Rain and wind strip the leaves from the trees, then the rain turns to snow before we can rake. We wind up shoveling leaves. It's just not right, and November knows it.

So do the kids. Sensing a November weakness in the parental will, they troop in after school and turn on the television. They know there's no use telling them to go outside and play. It's November. It's cold, gray, and wet. And since daylight savings time ended in October, it's getting dark, too.

Shakespeare's Richard III says, "Now is the winter of our discontent." Every November morning, the same thought is expressed less elegantly by thousands of Minnesotans waiting for the bus in the dark and the slush. November in Minnesota. Phooey. Somebody hand me my iPod. It's November. I'm going to download some Grieg.

Thanksgiving Road Game

FOR THE FIRST TIME in a long time, we'll be having Thanksgiving dinner at someone else's house this year—playing a road game. I'm not sure how I feel about it. It may actually be harder to be the company than it is to be the host.

There's the turkey recipe itself. It'll probably be fine; it just won't be the same. That goes for the dressing, too. I can live with the green bean casserole being different. But seriously, do you think they'd mind if I brought my own stuffing?

I'll miss our good china. It was my wife's grandmother's. Gramma Selma bought it (on the installment plan from a Sioux Falls department store, I'm guessing) back in the early part of the last century. That's a lot of Thanksgivings—tons of turkeys and potatoes and a whole bunch of plate passing ago—five generations' worth by my count. That's something to be grateful for.

Then there's the tryptophan—that ingredient in turkey that makes any uncle over forty-five go narcoleptic after dinner. At home, I usually fend off a nap by doing chores in the kitchen. But I'm a guest this year.

Is it bad form to push away from the table, wander over to someone else's couch, and pass out? It seems awkward at the very least. Even if I manage to stay awake, I won't be comfortable. There's a good chance I'll be sitting in my host's favorite football-watching spot. I hate sitting in another guy's spot. All those semiclose male friends and relatives will be sitting there too—guys who will want to talk politics or, worse yet, root for the Cowboys.

Dessert will come. Sugared-up kids will race around screaming. I'll start to send my wife those "let's go" vibes. She'll receive them, and just because she can, she'll stay an extra fifteen minutes for every vibe I send.

Eventually, though, she'll say it's time. The drive home will be starchy, salty, and semisilent, with occasional comments and grunts: so-and-so has put on weight; the such-and-suches are getting set in their ways. More semisilence will pass. We'll take in the first holiday lights of the season. Then I'll say, "Let's have Thanksgiving at our house next year."

A Thanksgiving Lesson

MOTHER IS IRISH — a teacher and librarian with one of those precise, diamond-hard, Irish intellects that encouraged the Jesuits to keep trying to educate the rest of us peat-digging churls for centuries. She put herself through teacher's college in the depths of the Depression, then after the war, for reasons she still doesn't quite understand, she got married and had nine kids.

Around our house back in the day, she turned everything into a teachable moment. And for quite a while the lesson was that "life isn't all fun and games, you know." She used to serve Thanksgiving dinner with a side order of admonition in the form of especially galling vegetables — yucky vegetables that looked as bad as they tasted.

There were Brussels sprout years and cauliflower years. Most memorable of all was the mashed rutabaga year. You know rutabaga — the dictionary defines it as "a brassicaceous plant having a yellow or white-fleshed, edible tuber." If "brassicaceous" means tasting like the fourth day of an untreated case of strep, the dictionary has it about right. Rutabaga is the only vegetable I know that ought to be seasoned with one or two large dashes of Absorbine Jr.

But there was the rutabaga on the table with the dressing and the turkey and all the fixings. There was no messing around; life wasn't all fun and games, you know. She made sure we all had rutabaga, come hell or high water. Meanwhile, next door at the Johnsons', the vegetables du jour were candied yams and marshmallow salad.

As Mother looked on, we reluctantly helped ourselves to the smallest possible portions and dutifully yagged the mashed rutabaga down with only one or two involuntary gag reflexes from a couple of the younger kids.

The ensuing years have proved Mother right. Life hasn't been all fun and games. On the whole, though, I'd say life has been pretty good. And this Thursday, sitting at the head of the table, I'll say a quick little prayer of thanks for my Irish mother, then nudge the twelve-year-old on my right. "Do me a favor, Sport," I'll say. "Pass the marshmallow salad."

An Amusing Pastime

THERE'S A BAR IN A SMALL TOWN on Lake Mille Lacs
with a picture window that looks out across Highway
169 at a huge bay of the big lake. In a week or two, only a
matter of days after the bay has iced over, the local folks
gathering in the bar after work will renew their age-old
tradition of watching the early season fools drive their
pickups out there on super-thin ice to fish at dusk.

You don't really know Minnesota until you've sat
there, surrounded by knotty pine and stuffed walleyes,
with neon beer signs coloring the deepening twilight,
listening to the locals critique their more adventurous
neighbors' thin-ice driving form while you nurse a long-
neck beer.

They consider you fainthearted if you hold the door
of your truck open in case you have to bail out. But it's
okay if you drive with the windows down.

Should you actually go through the ice, there is a
school of thought among some aficionados that says you
should ride the truck all the way down and then sit there

and contemplate the breadth and extent of your stupidity as icy water fills the cab.

I met a man who did just that. He said that, sitting there, water flowing in, he was amazed at just how flat the lake was as the ice passed eye level—that and the school of crappies suspended out there in the water ahead of his windshield.

It is, of course, no laughing matter. It's dangerous, and every year seems to produce at least one dire story about someone somewhere in Minnesota driving on the ice too early in the season. Sitting there, the locals don't so much laugh as look on and make small, quiet observations in half phrases.

"Well, there goes Larry."

Or "A little early for a three-quarter ton."

It's a tradition worthy of a *National Geographic* spread. In Pamplona, it's the running of the bulls through the streets. In Minnesota, they drive trucks on early season lake ice. All of which begs a timeless question: Where's Minnesota's Hemingway when we really need him?

North Country Fashion Statement

LET'S TALK NORTH WOODS FASHION. Let's talk bait shop attendants and guys with snowplows on their 4x4s. Small-engine repairmen and tow truck drivers. Men who make their living out in the woods. Guys with nicknames like "Ole" or "Swede." Guys with vise grips and screwdrivers and stray bolts and oily machine parts rolling around the foot wells of their trucks.

Not for these guys, the new autumn looks from the fashion runways of Paris. No, give them that classic Minnesota male winter look, the one that hasn't changed in half a century.

It starts with a long underwear shirt mottled with syrup or snuff stains. This wardrobe essential goes with your favorite pocket t-shirt and sets off that casually unbuttoned plaid work shirt. Blue jeans are de rigueur, of course, especially jeans with that saggy, unwashed, worn-every-day-for-a-week look. Jeans that are frayed at the knees and along the thighs to give the world a playful glimpse of long underwear.

In Paris or Akeley, shoes make the outfit. For early winter in Minnesota, we suggest a scuffed lace-up work boot worn untied, as if you just stepped into them to go outside and change propane tanks. A bit later in the season, in the big cold of January, you can go with an insulated boot if you like.

Outer wear? The classic Minnesota layered look features a thin quilted vest in maroon or green over a gray, hooded, zip-up sweatshirt. Add a winter jacket from your favorite snowmobile or all-terrain vehicle manufacturer and you're ready for a night on the town.

Top it all off with a classic blue stocking cap. Look for something in a synthetic fiber, such as Orlon. Accessorize with a rugged pair of old choppers and two weeks' worth of beard.

Voilà. You have achieved the Minnesota male winter look. You are ready for any social event Minnesota may throw at you, from breakfast with the guys at the Main Street Diner to a day at the garage or an evening in the fishing shack.

It doesn't get any more chic than this. Are the women of Minnesota lucky or what?

Winter Wimps

HAVE YOU NOTICED the wave of winter wimpification that's overrun Minnesota these past few decades? It's all this new technology, and global warming, too. People have forgotten what real winter is like, and I for one am darned nervous about it.

I'm not kidding. Two entire generations of Minnesotans have grown up without inheriting long underwear from their older brothers and sisters. I ask you—is that right? The same goes for wool socks and insulated boots. These days, you have to summon all your parental gumption just to make your high school kid take a winter coat to school. Not to wear it—just to take it. Just to carry it from the house to his buddy's fuel-injected, sure-to-start car.

Truthfully, why should the kid take the coat? Any fool can start these modern cars at a wimpy, globally warm, fifteen below. And the governor closes the schools if the thermometer flirts with minus twenty.

Starting a carbureted car at forty below zero—now

that was an art. You only had so much juice in the battery, and if you pumped the gas pedal too much you flooded it. My older brother explained it to me like this:

"Push it all the way to the floor and count to three. Then take your right foot and put it in the glove box."

And they make warm clothes so light and brightly colored now. They send you catalogs full of people who look suspiciously Californian—people who smile as they romp in the snow and model the latest styles.

Remember when real Minnesotans wore quilted green coveralls? Sears, Roebuck green, plus purple Orlon Vikings stocking caps? During warm spells—when it got up to zero—they slipped their upper torsos out of their coveralls, tied the arms around their waists and worked (not romped) in their long underwear shirts.

And they didn't smile. Cold weather was nothing to smile about.

In an antique store up on the Cuyuna Range recently, I came across three entire shelves of well-worn, cast-aside Hudson's Bay blankets. The kind you'd throw over the top of the quilt in a big cold snap. The kind you and The Wife would use to build a heat island as you lay there together in the dark and listened to the house crack from the cold. Antiques. Hudson Bay blankets in Minnesota in winter. *Antiques.*

The polar ice caps are melting. Greenland is emerging from under its glaciers. If that's not warm enough for you, you can probably buy Thinsulate-filled jockey shorts made in China down at Wal-Mart.

Me? I want Minnesota winter back the way it was— unwimpy. A monthlong Siberian cold snap would put a spring in my step and a melody in my heart and start to get the entire state back to cold, miserable normal.

Together Again for the Holidays

THE HOLIDAYS are upon us again, that magical time of the year when the family gathers to open all the presents and reopen the political wounds from the campaign just past. The brother-in-law who is especially sensitive to political schadenfreude, for example. He was a McCain man, and he was spoiling for a fight when he arrived for Thanksgiving dinner. His coat hadn't reached the bed in the spare bedroom before he declared the president-elect an emperor and stated emphatically that this new emperor would bankrupt the country.

To the family's great credit, no one—neither Democrat nor Republican—would engage him on the subject. People raised their eyebrows and bit their lips and secretly smiled to one another, which only served to frustrate the man that much more. Eventually, he walled himself off at the far end of the living room couch after dinner and sat in icy silence watching football and seething.

Poor guy. He grew up in one of those blue-collar, Republican working families. I'll bet that, at Thanksgiving at his house when he was a kid, his old man would say a prayer of thanks that the New Deal was over and Eisenhower was in.

Now here he was, ensconced in late middle age, depressed at the prospect of four years of a Democratic administration that's beginning to feel like another New Deal, and here it was Thanksgiving. And no one in the family—not the screaming liberals, not the Republican business tycoons, no one—would give him a political opening.

It's a Minnesota thing, of course. A variation on a theme by Minnesota Nice. If you can't say anything nice on a holiday, go sit over there and keep your piehole shut. Let the resentment build. You'll need it later in the year.

For a minute or two, sitting there, surrounded by in-laws and noisy cousins, I considered asking him what he thought about the recount in the Coleman-Franken race. It would have been an act of charity. It would have given him the chance to vent. But then I thought better of it.

"Nah," I said to myself. "That one's got 'Do not open till Christmas' written all over it."

Sulking in a Winter Wonderland

THIS TIME OF YEAR, some Minnesotans tend to romanticize the holidays a bit. From now through New Year's, they've got a dose of Currier and Ives and an Irving Berlin holiday song for everyone. They gin up a winter wonderland full of happy-faced snowmen, sleigh bells, hot chocolate at skating parties, Dickensian ghosts of Christmases past, and shoppers rushing home with their treasures.

That's fine if you need to muster warm fuzzy feelings to fend off seasonal affective disorder. But a more practical, more Minnesotan approach might be to forego the warm fuzzies and embrace the colder, more reality-based aspects of winter and celebrate them as symbols of the real season and who we really are.

Those icy chunks that build up in car wheel wells, for example. The ones that fall off, freeze to the ground, and nearly break your toe when you try to kick them out of the way. Where's the Irving Berlin song about them? Or that first little trickle of cold, dirty water seeping into your shoe as you tiptoe through one of those gutter puddles that's too big to step over. Why can't that be one of your favorite things? Who needs snowflakes on mittens?

"Through the years we all will be together," goes one of the old Christmas songs, "if the Fates allow." It's a nice sentiment, but in real Minnesota this time of year, the kind of togetherness the Fates allow is more apt to be the kind you experience on a crowded, super-heated-yet-somehow-slushy rush hour bus. Or down at the impound lot after a snow emergency.

We are a practical and undemonstrative people. This time of year, we rise in the dark, work all day, and come home again in the dark. It's not a great routine, but it's our routine. We glean cultural cohesion from it, and somehow, those of us who can't quite get with the warm fuzzies of the holidays should embrace and celebrate the glorious, cold, drab ordinariness of it.

As for the happy holiday crowd, go ahead and celebrate as warmly and fuzzily as you want. Far be it from us, the less emotive, to rain on your parade. Then again, if it rained, they'd almost certainly have to cancel the Holidazzle Parade, wouldn't they?

A Christmas Shopping Memory

MY WORK TAKES ME OUTSTATE now and then, and the other week I found myself walking down a small-town Main Street with its stores and streetlights all decked out for the holidays. It was snowing, and I was suddenly transported back to a Christmas before Wal-Mart or mall stores, a Christmas when the stores along another Main Street were all I had.

It was freshman year of high school. There was this girl I kind of liked, although I had never spoken to her. For reasons I don't understand to this day, I felt obligated to buy her something. All those feelings and hormones were surging, and I had no idea what to do with them. Had it been a year earlier, I could have just punched her in the arm hard when we passed in the hall. But I was a high school man now. And now I needed—really needed—to use the last of my summer lawn-mowing money to buy her something.

The perfume counter at the drugstore seemed like a good place to start. But the drugstore smelled like my grandfather's foot powder. And in spite of names like

"Evening In Paris" and "Chanel Number Five," the perfumes smelled like the local funeral parlor. I moved on.

I wandered down the dime store gift aisle, looking for something in my price range. But the wife half of the husband-and-wife team who owned the store had chosen all the Christmas merchandise. She was well past fifty. My tastes were running vaguely hot. Hers were decidedly hot flashy. There was nothing. I moved on.

At the record store, I searched bins of 45s looking for one that expressed how I felt. Like my hormones, they ran the gamut from sultry to stupid. The right song just wasn't there.

I finally settled on a rack for 45 RPM records—a little ceramic dog with a coiled wire body. The records were supposed to fit between the coils. It was the stupidest thing I think I have ever seen, but I took it home secretly—and secretly wrapped it. And the next day at school, I walked up and handed it to her.

"This is for you," I said. "Merry Christmas." And I never spoke to her again.

Now It Can Be Christmas

UNCLE FRANK WORKED NIGHTS in a steel plant, so it was understandable that he looked owly when he and Aunt Babe and all those girl cousins joined Aunt Gick and Uncle Hank and their boys, and Aunt Pat and Uncle Red and their kids, at our house for dinner on Christmas Day.

Frank had shocky hair and a vaguely distracted look—like Stan Laurel—and a concave posture that was accentuated when he stood there with his hands in his pockets, surveying the noisy reunion of cousins as the coats got collected and dumped on a bed in a back bedroom. The chaos was exquisite but short-lived. Before long, the cousins would quiet down a little or disappear to other corners of the house. His wife would join her sisters in the kitchen. His brothers-in-law would take seats in the living room to smoke and talk, and Frank would sit down at the piano.

He would run through all the traditional Christmas fare—"Silent Night," "Jingle Bells," "The First Noel"—that sort of thing. Then he would wander off into popular Christmas tunes like "White Christmas,"

"I'll Be Home for Christmas," "Silver Bells," and what-have-you.

He played with a big, rolling left hand that bounced like a couple of heavyset aunts dancing a schottische with each other at a wedding. He sprayed the right hand notes over the top, adding plenty of sustain pedal to make it all ring. It was as if one of those barroom piano players in a western movie had suddenly launched into a medley of Tin Pan Alley holiday fare.

Eventually, he would run out of Christmas tunes. He would pause for a minute, light a cigarette, stare off into space, then turn back to the piano and, squinting through the cigarette smoke, he would begin a mazurka variation of Irving Berlin's "Easter Parade."

And then it could be Christmas. Then all was right with the world. Somehow, that Easter song written by a Russian Jewish immigrant and played by a Polish American uncle in the din of a large Irish American family reunion with no one really paying attention came to represent all that is good and happy about Christmas for me.

Since those days, I've spent Christmas in war zones and Christmas with strangers. I've spent a Christmas or two alone—and more than a few in the crowded happiness of my wife's extended family. But over the years, I've developed a resistance to the hype and the hustle. Christmas has become little more than retailers tugging at my heartstrings en route to my wallet.

All that would change in an instant though if just once—at a mall or on one of those radio stations that play Christmas music round the clock or maybe on an elevator Muzak holiday tape — they would slip in a piano solo, an almost polka version of Irving Berlin's "Easter Parade." Heavy on the left hand and the sustain pedal.

Alas, Poor Taurus

OUR '93 FORD TAURUS departed this vale of tears last week. One of the kids hit a patch of ice driving home from Madison and spun out on the Interstate just east of Menomonie. No one was hurt, but the Taurus was totaled, and I have been in a kind of low-grade fatherly mourning ever since.

I loved that car. I loved it with a passion that only a parent with young drivers can truly understand. Sure, it was ugly. I could feel waves of disapproval radiating from behind the neighbors' drawn drapes whenever one of the kids brought it home from school and parked it on the street for a day or two.

But it was paid for. It had less than a hundred thousand miles on the odometer. The brakes were good. The tires had another thirty thousand miles on them. It didn't burn oil. The insurance was reasonable. That car survived four years of the high school parking lot and three years of college capers, the details of which it's best I not know. In an age when your kids' friends show up in a cavalcade of anonymous, worn, rusty old Corollas or

Civics or family minivans on their way out, that Taurus had earned respect from kids and parents alike.

It was like an old, loyal, half-blind family dog—so much so that when another one of the kids did sixteen hundred dollars' worth of damage to it a while back, I paid to have it repaired. I just wasn't ready to put it down.

Now it's gone. Tears well up just thinking about it.

Some cars you get attached to. Some you don't. I still miss a certain very used crème-over-pink '55 Oldsmobile Holiday Coupe I owned ever so briefly more than three decades ago.

On the other hand, I once sold an unlovable '57 Plymouth for five dollars and an all-you-can-eat fish dinner at Perkins in St. Cloud—good riddance, pass the tartar sauce.

The '93 Taurus that died three miles east of Exit 41 in Wisconsin last week was one of the greats in my book. And since tomorrow is New Year's Eve, this will forever be the year we lost the Taurus.

Dog Days in the Ice Fishing Shack

JANUARY IN THE ICE FISHING SHACK. The walleyes and crappies have quit biting. The big northerns, too. The big cold weather is here, and game fish of all kinds have assumed a fickle ambivalence even toward suckers and fathead minnows, the most tempting of all live bait.

From Lake of the Woods and the other famous ice fishing venues to the local lake in the middle of town, men, driven out of the house by wives who've had more than enough, hunker over holes in the ice, twitching their bobbers, reduced to coaxing half-hearted bites from sluggish perch and bluegills—species they wouldn't bother to fish for at all in July. Tedium has set in with a vengeance, and this wasn't exactly a thrill-a-minute proposition in the first place.

A cold northwest wind blows. The small stove ticks wispy, propane-scented heat into the drafty little space. Icy silence reigns. The bobber mesmerizes. You enter a no-mind state that would have cost forty bucks to acquire in a Tuesday night community education meditation course.

"How deep you fishin'?" your buddy asks.

The words echo on some transcendental plane. "Yes," you ask yourself. "How deep *am* I fishing?"

Your mind starts to play tricks on you. Cribbage becomes intellectually stimulating. Beer seems like a good idea. Gas station beef jerky as tough as rawhide is suddenly haute cuisine.

These are the dog days of ice fishing. The fish, not biting, are suspended a foot off the bottom. The fishermen, dangling bait, are suspended in their shacks overhead. Everything and everyone is waiting in frigid futility for ice fishing season to come to a merciful end.

Your buddy thinks there may be a flurry of action around sunset, but your heart isn't in it. Your heart is at home. In the recliner with the remote control. But she won't let you come home. Not yet.

Maybe after sunset.

The Inscrutable Finn

A FRIEND OF MINE up around Brainerd, a third-gener-
ation Finnish American with Iron Range roots, is in the
middle of producing a coffee-table book about saunas
(he says "sow-nah," I say "saw-nah"). He spent most of
June in Finland taking photos of old saunas. As long as
he was there, he took quite a few saunas himself.

He describes each old sauna lovingly—rever-
ently—as if it were some sort of subarctic version of
Lourdes. One, the oldest, was little more than a hole in
the side of a hill with a stovepipe protruding from the
ground a few feet above the door.

As a fourth-generation Irish American, I don't see
the appeal—for the book or for saunas in general. I'm
inhibited. If there is sweating to be done, my genes say
do it fully clothed, preferably standing at the bar in a pub
over a pint of Guinness, certainly not naked in the pres-
ence of other people. My contours, my sweat, and my
cellulite are my business—mine alone.

Once, when the neighbors invited us over to sit in their
hot tub, I said we had a family function to go to. Then I

sat in the basement with the shades pulled until bedtime.

We Irish may be inhibited, but those Finns are downright bipolar. Summers of midnight sun and winters of absolute darkness have induced a giddy melancholia in them. They think sitting naked with the neighbors in an overheated outhouse in a stand of scrubby popple trees out by the pond behind the barn is a celebration of culture.

No wonder then, that from northeastern Minnesota, across northern Wisconsin, and eastward across Michigan's Upper Peninsula, the descendants of other European cultures raise their eyebrows and adopt a knowing tone whenever they talk about Finlanders. From Ely to Sault St. Marie, few subcultures are thought to be as ingenious, as industrious, as intelligent and educated—or as eccentric.

No self-respecting Iron Range or north woods Swede, Norwegian, Serb, Croat, Slovenian, or Italian can drive by a Finnish neighbor's place without sneaking a peek to see what they're up to over there.

And what my Finnish American friend is up to is a book about "sow-nahs." A coffee-table book, thank goodness. You can't read anything in a sauna. Not even the newspaper. The sweat gets in your eyes and rolls off the end of your nose. It plops on the page, pulps up the paper, and ruins everything.

I am sure that, in true Finlander form, my friend's book will be beautiful, the photos will be glorious, and the text will be evocative. It will be almost glorious and evocative enough to make me want to take a "sow-nah"—but not quite.

Crows

IT'S THE TIME OF YEAR when the crows get together late in the afternoon and fly wingtip to wingtip in big formations that seem to stretch from horizon to horizon. It's as if a ragged, flapping motorcycle gang suddenly left the pavement and took to the air.

A little Internet research will tell you that they're getting together to roost for the night, which they do routinely in winter. Somewhere, a couple of trees are about to turn into a hopelessly overbooked hotel for crows.

Looking up into a late afternoon winter sky and seeing hundreds, even thousands of crows flying in a formation that would do the Eighth Air Force proud, you can't help but think they're up to something. They look like they're on a mission or like a mob with a purpose going off to perpetrate mayhem somewhere.

They're usually quiet as they pass overhead. Whatever they have been bickering about all afternoon has been resolved. They're in absolute agreement now, and they look like they mean business.

Other birds will fly in a flock, too. For example, you'll see starlings in big flights over farm fields. But flights of starlings seem as mindless as schools of fish. They swoop and climb and swirl and change direction for no apparent reason at all. Individual birds disappear in the roil of the flock.

Crows, on the other hand, remain individuals. Something in the slower, more deliberate flap of their wings differentiates them from one another as the entire group moves across the sky. Throw in the colors—the black of the crows, the darkening blue of the sky, the white of the snow, and the red of the sun on its way to the western horizon—and you have one of those simple-yet-spectacular displays of nature that just affirm things somehow.

There is something almost Lenten about it. Looking up, you can sense the cycle of the seasons changing. You can't quite see spring from down here, but maybe the crows can from their Mardi Gras parade up there.

Whatever you're doing, you have to pause, look up, and admire—even envy—them. There you are, fixed to the frozen earth. There they are, flapping across the late afternoon sky, celebrating the pure, simple glory of being crows.

Real World Valentine's Day

T. S. ELIOT says April is the cruelest month. I say it's February. Specifically, that part of February pertaining to Valentine's Day. Here we are, human beings, less than perfect, working hard to get by, and here is this day, hyped by retailers and greeting card manufacturers, on which we are supposed to celebrate some idealized, stereotypical concept of love.

In Valentine's Day commercials, beautiful people give one another perfect gifts. Diamonds. Toiletries. Expensive lingerie. They exchange cards, which they read with melodramatic ardor as if they were Robert and Elizabeth Browning.

In the real world, we are more apt to give one another the flu than diamonds. Cards come from the gas station, not from the heart. And that off-the-rack lingerie always fits less than perfectly, revealing parts of our anatomies and libidos that probably ought to stay covered up. In the real world, we are less like classic lovers than we are like bruised fruit in a bin down at the grocery store. We show what love we can by being understanding and accepting each other, bruises and all.

Donald Rumsfeld once observed that you go to war with the army you have and not the one you want. In real world affairs of the heart, something like the exact opposite occurs. You fall in love with the one you want and over time, a bruise, a flaw, or a foible at a time, you discover who you really have.

Unlike love in commercials or in romantic fiction, love in the real world plays out not against vast vistas and epic events but against the backdrop of everyday life. In the real world, you show your undying love by taking the garbage can to the curb on trash day. Or tending that mousetrap in the pantry. Or saying, "I'll do the dishes. You go relax."

But then Valentine's Day happens. Advertisers do their damnedest to equate love with getting stuff. The idealists among us hop on the bandwagon, and pretty soon we're all expecting perfection. And when the object of our affection either cannot or will not (or simply does not) come across with the perfect gift or the perfect evening, Valentine's Day, like Christmas, ends in vague disappointment with some of us feeling less than perfectly loved.

Cruel February. Stupid Cupid. How much better it would be for all of us to revel in the imperfect and everyday aspects of love. Love among unbalanced checkbooks and unexpected car trouble. Love that falls asleep on the sofa before the ten o'clock news. Love that, contrary to Saint Paul, isn't always patient or kind and tends to instruct the beloved in his shortcomings as a driver.

That's love in the real world. That's what I'll be celebrating imperfectly with a certain someone this February 14—just like we celebrate it every other day. Here's hoping you have someone to celebrate real world imperfect love with, too.

A Timeless Saga

THERE'S SOMETHING TIMELESS about getting an ice fishing house off a Minnesota lake when it's frozen in. It's a saga that takes a lifetime to appreciate.

In the beginning, you're young, strong, impetuous, and prone to use brute force to break the shack free from the ice. Only later do you grasp the fundamental wisdom of opening your wallet, extracting forty bucks, and having a couple of impetuous young guys with an old 4x4 truck bust it out and haul it away for you.

I'm not talking about those new-fangled, factory-made fish houses with generators and microwave ovens and satellite TVs. With those babies, you just drop down a set of wheels and tow them away. I'm talking about an old fashioned, homemade ice fishing shack on 2x6 skids. The kind you build in the garage in October, drag out on the lake in December, and come to terms with at this time of year, when the skids are frozen three inches into the ice.

The quiet and serenity were exquisite in January. Back then, the shack was a fishy-smelling monastery cell worthy of a Trappist monk. There was nothing but the sound of the wind, the ticking heat of the stove, the hiss of the white gas lantern, and an occasional twitch of the bobber to disrupt your meditation.

Now though, your piscatorial Shangri-la has become a rather acute pain in the neck. Not only is it frozen in hard, but if you don't remove it, the Department of Natural Resources will burn it to the ice. And the more you try to bust it out, the more you're tempted to hand them the gas can and matches.

The right tool for the job is an ice chisel—about three pounds of steel wedge welded to the end of a four-foot steel pole. It's a blunt piece of work. If you come from peasant stock, a few minutes with an ice chisel will put you in touch with your roots. You chop away at the ice that's built up along the sides of the skids. But even after you've chopped all the ice away from the sides, the bottoms of the skids are still frozen to the lake.

You tug. You pry. You discover new and unusual combinations of scatological gerunds. Eventually, you're reduced to a panting heap of humanity, on all fours on the ice, promising never, ever to do this again.

At this point, the two young guys with the old 4x4 appear. Your wallet comes out of your pocket. Two twenties come out of your wallet. Your ice fishing shack comes out of the ice ruts and gets towed to its summer home in the weeds behind the reed bed at the edge of the lake.

It's a timeless seasonal saga. One that plays out over and over again. Ice fishing shacks rise. Ice fishing shacks sink into disrepair and decay in the weeds. Today's young bucks with 4x4s become tomorrow's old guys with open wallets. Like stinging snow on the wind of a March blizzard, it all comes and goes.

Except for the Department of Natural Resources. The Department of Natural Resources lasts forever.

Split-level Shack-whacky

I AM IRISH. Every year about this time, something deep in my genes produces an image of some ancestral couple—my great-great-great-great-grandparents or more—squatting in a rock hovel, staring at one another across a peat-smudgy fire, looking at the dwindling pile of potatoes, and wondering if spring will ever really arrive. It's these early spring snowstorms. They smother hope and release your inner peasant to brood and plot against anyone with whom you have lived all winter—anyone. This time of year, people flat-out get on your nerves.

As I write this, I am secretly plotting against my eleven-year-old. Somewhere back in January, someone brought home one of those heavy vinyl exercise balls, and he has developed a habit of dribbling it the length and breadth of the living room.

Dribbling incessantly. Tell him to stop, and he will for a moment. Then he will absent-mindedly start dribbling again. Dribbling...dribbling...dribbling.

I would tell him to go outside. I would tell him to go find some friend and go sledding. These days, though, kids don't go outside and sled. They stay inside and play video games, especially during heavy, wet, spring snowstorms that sog up their snow pants and make any trip to a sliding hill more like a trip to an iceberg-themed water park.

So I sit, remote control on the arm of the sofa, mind functioning at a low drone, struggling to watch television around a large, bouncing blue ball. I tried pointing the remote at both the boy and the ball and clicking the off button. No soap. The boy continues to dribble. The ball continues to bounce. I suggested sports and after-school activity programs. Again no soap. This is our fourth child. He is wise to such tricks.

What needs to happen here is for the ball to have an unfortunate accident. An aneurysm in the vinyl—or better yet, just a flat-out rupture. It can't disappear completely, though: this late in winter the boy is wary, brooding, and suspicious too. He would know I was behind it. A nick with a butcher knife would do the trick. Maybe then I could convince him the dog bit the ball.

I sit. I plot. Any of a thousand other ways to get rid of the ball go through my head. Beyond the bouncing blue ball, the television weather reporter is telling me more snow is on the way.

I clutch at the remote control. I click. I brood. I plot.

Contemplating Gutter Gloves

DIRTY, DENTED HUBCAPS. Lost disposable lighters. Scratched-off lottery tickets. Grit. Litter. Chewed gum. Wadded tissues that fell from purses and pockets as people fished up coins to plug parking meters months ago.

As snowbanks melt all over town, strange ugly stuff is blossoming on sidewalks and streets everywhere. Stuff to meditate upon as long as you keep your mind in the gutter.

For me, most compelling of all are those winter-flat gutter gloves. Fashionable leather gloves, rubberized work gloves, cheap gloves, expensive gloves, gloves of all sizes and styles lying there, dirty, wet, and (most of all) flat.

Who owned all those gloves? Where are the owners now? A gutter glove is a sad little metaphor, a half story, half told, with a flat, soggy moral lying somewhere nearby and a clean, dry, never-again-to-be-paired mate waiting at home alone in a basket by the front door. A winter-flat gutter glove can never go home again. Even if it could, it would never be the same as the glove that wasn't lost. It would have suffered and endured so much more.

See what I mean? Winter-flat gutter gloves don't just drip gutter water. They drip cruel, cold, bitter irony, too.

On city park sidewalks and along suburban walking trails, people find mittens all the time. They pick them up and hang them from branches or leave them on benches, thinking the owners will come back for them. But nobody picks up gutter gloves. Nobody hangs them from nearby meters or drapes them atop the mailbox at the corner. And nobody ever comes back for them. Gutter gloves lie where they fell, bleak, somber, soggy, and sullen as Lent.

Then spring comes, early crocuses appear, and city workers (some wearing work gloves) come along, posting signs that say "No Parking This Block Tomorrow." When tomorrow comes, so does a big Public Works street sweeper. The grit and the dirt and the dreck and the winter-flat gutter gloves get swept up and hauled away to be forgotten—as forgotten as a dead great-uncle who didn't include you in his will.

But it's only late winter. The gutter gloves are still out there, just emerging from snowbanks and coming out of hibernation. Blossoming.

Should you encounter one somewhere today, don't touch it (good lord, your mother would never want you to touch it). Just pause for a moment and contemplate it. Use it as a springboard to think about the transient nature of human existence for a moment.

Then mutter "Winter-flat gutter glove—yuck" and get going. Time's wasting. You haven't got all day.

Thinking Ill of the Literate

AN OLD FRIEND INVITED ME to join her book club last week. I don't know. I've been in book clubs before, and I'm not sure I want to be in one again. Book club members are forever overreaching: choosing too much book, something way too cerebral, a "classic," or something pretentiously important and virtually unreadable.

There's a fine line between important and boring. Book club selections are on the wrong side of that line just about every time. And the weightier the book, the more likely it becomes that someone in the club will decide they're an expert on it—or the subject matter or the era or the author.

Lucky you. Now you not only have a boring book, you also have a boring expert who's loaded for bear. And the dynamics of most book club meetings are such that someone always enables the expert of the month, providing whatever stimulus the expert needs to blather on and on and on.

Sometimes it's a simple question. Sometimes it's an opposing point of view. It doesn't matter. The result is always the same: a long, tedious back-and-forth between the expert and the enabler while everyone else sits there in that dark, after-supper, weeknight funk. No one else contributes because no one else can. They're not prepared. They procrastinated. They didn't start reading the book until after the kids went to bed last night.

The book club. She wants me to join the book club. I'll feel so guilty if I don't say yes. Don't Minnesota's Official Rules and Bylaws state that if I say no and they decide to disband the club it will be my fault for not joining?

So I guess I'll join. I guess I have to. Yish. Now watch. The first book is going to be *Finnegans Stinking Wake*.

Jogging Again

WITH SPRING ON THE WAY and a winter's worth of white carbohydrates on my hips, I'm thinking of taking up jogging again. Somebody please stop me before I start.

It will take months to build up any stamina. It will be weeks before I can maintain so much as a shuffling pace. Even in peak condition, I won't so much jog as lurch along the city's pedestrian paths, passing no one except for those old couples tottering along with their tube socks and fanny packs and clip-on sunglasses.

There was a time when I could get up in the morning, run seven miles, then bicycle downtown to work. I wasn't world-class, but I wasn't bad. I could negotiate the city's neighborhoods with more-or-less effortless élan, taking in the scenery, enjoying that elusive runner's high.

Back then, the theme songs from *Chariots of Fire* and *Rocky* looped in my head. I could stretch out my stride, pick up the pace, and pretend for a block or two that I was some sort of distance runner kicking for the finish line.

Now, though, assuming I work my way back into shape, there will be no kicking. There will be only that litany of pain as my body and I revisit the sites of so many activity-related injuries. There is the ankle I sprained backpacking in Idaho—still stiff and sore all these years later. And the high school football knee that's gone bone-on-bone now. And the combination hip and lower-back compression, permanently wrenched thanks to a youth misspent in landscaping. Even the surgically repaired shoulder, a souvenir of all that pickup basketball in the park, will register a twinge or two.

So, no sir. No kicking. I'll stick with that spooky, semigingerly old-guy pace. And no more "Chariots of Fire" playing in my head. Just a semirhythmic recitation of grunts and groans—a kind of "ooh-unh-ouch-unh-oop-oop-ouch" as I all but tiptoe to ease up on the joints.

As for wardrobe, it will be the same as it was in high school—gray sweatpants, the baggier the better, and an old gray hooded sweatshirt so maybe the neighbors won't know it's me. I will accessorize the look with liniment and miscellaneous old braces and Ace bandages from the Peter Smith Collection of Support Devices. The bandages have lost a bit of elasticity over the years, but what the hell—so have I.

I'll start training as soon as the paths thaw. It will be in the early morning under cover of darkness. I see no need to humiliate myself in broad daylight. In fact, this year, I think I'll do all my jogging before sunrise. It's a nice time of day. I can't scare small children then.

If you sleep with the windows open, keep an ear out for my footsteps. You'll be able to tell it's me by the muted "ooh-unh-ouch-ouch" and that faint hint of liniment on the cool, predawn spring breeze.

Talk about Your Golf Drives

EVERY YEAR ABOUT THIS TIME, two Minnesota species come out of hibernation. The black bear wakes up hungry and grumpy and ready to eat anything. But hungry bears are sweetness and light compared to the winter-starved Minnesota golfer.

There are upper-crust golfers among us—country clubbers who, recession be damned, jet off, clubs and all, for a midwinter golf fix and come back all tan and happy and glib. Then there are the rest of us poor shlubs—real Minnesotans who have been swinging snow shovels instead of seven irons.

It's March. We're getting antsy to get in some golf. Weekend after weekend, TV has tormented us with tournaments where people in polo shirts (and sweaters if it's chilly) make beautifully precise shots on impeccably manicured, incredibly beautiful courses from San Diego to Monterey to Los Angeles. Now the pro tour has moved to Florida and, next month, up into Georgia for the Masters.

Meanwhile, we remain snowbound. It's not fair. It's not right. While some of us console ourselves with a trip to the golf dome to hit balls off Astroturf into a big plastic tarp, others need—really need—to be outside in fresh air on real grass, preferably grass growing out of unfrozen ground.

So every year about this time, while birds migrate north, real Minnesota golfers migrate south down 35W in search of the first open course. Some years, it's as close as Des Moines. Others, it's the far side of Kansas City. Wherever it is, when a real Minnesota golfer spots the first flag on the first green of the first open course, that's when spring starts, even if it's forty degrees and raining.

There can be snowdrifts in the sand traps and ice on the water hazards. It can be one of those flat, dull, low-self-esteem roadside courses you wouldn't think of playing in May. Who cares? It's golf, real golf.

Walking into the clubhouse, you can count on three things: The course will be empty—completely devoid of locals. The guy behind the counter will be changing the sign, bumping the rates up from last year. And at some point as you happily pay, he'll ask, "You're from Minnesota, aren't you?"

Cooking with Grandma

WHENEVER I HEAR one of those food poisoning stories
come across the radio, I reach over and turn the volume
up. It's only a matter of time until my mother-in-law is
implicated. She's developed a cavalier attitude toward
freshness codes lately. She thinks they're a sign that
America has gone soft. She says common sense and her
nose will tell her when something goes bad.

It's the South Dakota Depression-era farm girl in her,
the one who grew up without electricity, refrigeration,
or pasteurization. Either that or it's the frugal Fridley
mother of eight, who routinely performed miracles with
loaves of Wonder bread and cans of tuna fish and got her
lunchtime multitudes fed.

There was a brief period, a couple of decades, when she
cooked fairly normally. Now she's reverting to form, paring
the spongy parts off shriveled potatoes and making soup
with octogenarian leftovers. She's playing fast and loose
with the microbes and reminding us every so often that
Fleming developed penicillin from some form of mold.

"Eat this," I once heard her say as she handed an open

container of cottage cheese to a grandchild. "Then I'll tell you how old it is."

She's even found stores that specialize in selling old and dented canned goods with missing labels. She's come home with bags full of God-knows-what and a glow in her heart that not even the most successful Blooming-dale's bargain hunter could hope to match.

The woman doesn't date freshness in days or weeks—or even months. It's a matter of years, decades, and now centuries—even millennia. There was the can of coconut milk she bought in Hawaii in 1976, last seen on a cupboard shelf in 2002. Asked where it went, she said she'd made cookies with it and served the cookies to her card club.

"The ladies said they were the best they'd ever had," she reported smugly.

Don't get me wrong. The woman is a great cook. She still makes a world-class gingersnap, and I'll put her fried chicken up against anyone's, anytime and anywhere. But like Ronald Reagan negotiating with the Soviet Union, I've adopted a trust-but-verify stance when she cooks. I like my chicken—all my food for that matter—to be at least four decades younger than I am. I want to see it every step of the way from the store to her frying pan and onto my plate.

I'm going to keep an eye on my mother-in-law. I suggest you keep an eye on yours, too. Those old recipes are great—especially with fresh ingredients. Which is why, if I have my say, Sunday dinner will be at our house again this week.

Are You with Us?
Or Are You One of Them?

THERE IS A VAST SCHISM among people who fish for crappies in Minnesota in the spring: either you fish from a boat or you fish from shore. Which side you're on says a lot about you.

Personally, I throw in with the shore-fishing crowd. Fishing boats with their GPS systems and fish finders and trolling motors and aerated live wells have gotten way too high-tech and cushy for me. Fish finders, phooey.

If you fish from shore you find fish by driving the road at the edge of the lake and keeping an eye on the phone wire overhead. Find a snargle of miscast hooks and bobbers hanging from the wire, and you've found the fish. And people who fish from shore don't need all that other hoity-toity stuff either. If you can't buy it at the bait shop or gas station, you don't need it.

Which isn't to say there aren't one or two essentials. A five-gallon pail, for example. It holds the crappies you catch and, covered with a musty old boat cushion, serves as a place to sit.

Shore fishing is much more egalitarian than fishing from a boat, too. Ethnicity, education, and socioeconomic status melt away. Start catching crappies and people up and down the shore gravitate toward you. Their bobbers magically drift closer to yours.

We shore fishers pull for one another. When you have a fish on, you have a cheering section who'll be there for you even if the unthinkable should happen and your fish turns out to be a bullhead—or worse yet, a dogfish—instead of a crappie.

It's Us versus Them. You sit there on your bucket, working your spot and looking at a boatload of rich guys—maybe even an outdoor writer or two—who buzz over and anchor thirty yards off shore to work the spot, too.

"No-good cake-eaters," you mutter.

But only in spring. Soon the days will get longer. The sunlight will get stronger. The crappies will move off into summer feeding patterns. The rich guys and outdoor writers in their boats will move off to fish for other species and to write other stories. The fish-crappies-from-shore/fish-crappies-from-boat schism will recede until next year.

Trust me, though. The schism is eternal. A thousand springs from now, some future Minnesota shore fisher will drive along the edge of some lake, spot a snargle of hooks and bobbers hanging from the wire overhead, and think, "This is the spot. I think I'll try it here."

And three rich guys in a boat—possibly even a future outdoor writer—will motor over and drop anchor right next to him.

No-good cake-eaters.

Planting Corn

APRIL IN MINNESOTA. The sun is getting stronger, the soil is getting warmer, and in cities and towns all over the state, people who grew up on farms—former Future Farmers of America—are getting a far-off look in their eyes as they think about home and planting corn.

You can take the kid off the farm. The kid can go to college and from there to work in the big city. But you can't take the farm out of the kid. This time of year, looking out the office window, seeing that first tinge of green in the trees, former Future Farmers of America tend to go slightly bipolar—to hurtle between a nostalgia for farm life and a gratitude that says, "Thank God I don't have to do *that* anymore."

Planting corn was hard work. You missed two weeks of school. If you weren't on a tractor disking, dragging, or plowing, you were doing your regular chores plus picking up the slack for someone who was out working the fields. You did a little of everything and a lot of some things. The only thing you didn't do was actually plant the corn. That was the old man's job.

It had to be planted just so, and the rows had to be even and straight. It was no job for a boy. There was a certain amount of keeping up with the Joneses in planting straight rows; when all that corn germinated, everyone driving by would be able to see just what kind of farmer the old man really was.

Then there was that hole in your adolescent social life—no dating, no dances, no school sports, no fun. To those of us who grew up in town, it sounded like a combination of child labor and boot camp with farm parents acting as slave drivers, prison guards, and drill instructors.

Still, it's April. Planting season. And out in farm country, a new generation of farmers and farm kids equipped with computers, GPS systems, genetically tuned seeds, and a new generation of equipment are starting to get this year's crop in the ground. And here in town, old farm kids are looking homeward.

So if you see a former Future Farmer of America standing at the window, looking out toward that ever-so-slightly green horizon at the edge of the city, walk over and put your arm around his shoulder. As sympathetically as possible, tell him, "I know, buddy, I know."

Then give him a nudge in the ribs and say, "Thank God you don't have to do *that* any more, hunh?"

A Little Frugality, Por Favor

WALL STREET IS REELING. The politicians are bobbing and weaving. Wide-bottomed, shifty-eyed corporate CEOs are testifying before committees on Capitol Hill, and financial storm clouds are roiling on the horizon. Maybe it's time we Minnesotans turned around and asked our family elders if they have any insights or advice about coping with hard times.

You know the elders I'm talking about. People like Uncle Elwin, who developed a skill for getting the most out of a pair of shoes during the Depression. He saved up and bought a good set of oxfords and had eight sets of heels and five sets of half soles put on them rather than break down and shell out for a new pair. People who have long-lost values and skills that may come in handy again sooner than we think.

There are still women among us who used to set aside a day and bake the seven or eight loaves of bread it would take to get the family through a week of meals back in the 1950s. Good bread. The kind of bread that, warm from the oven, properly sliced and buttered, could get an hour's worth of yard work out of an otherwise shiftless boy.

There are still people among us who know how to plan, dig, and plant a vegetable garden and tend it from the first radish of June through the last squash of October. Woe unto any rabbit that might drop by to browse—those old-timers haven't forgotten the recipe for rabbit stew.

"I don't want to say we were poor," an old guy up near Fort Ripley told me a while back. "But we hunted for game back during the Depression. When we ran out of game, we hunted for squirrels. When we ran out of squirrels—well, let's just say I know what robin tastes like."

Given our yuppified lifestyle we wouldn't call it "robin." We'd probably call it "lawn squab."

We hail from a long line of frugal people—from string savers and sock darners and trouser patchers and World War II aluminum, tin, and paper drive veterans. Somewhere down there, past the credit card bills and the 401(k) statements, we've got that stubborn, self-reliant gumption gene and a firm belief that not even this hellish combination of greedy corporate CEOs and Dagwood Bumstead–class elected officials can screw things up so badly that we can't roll up our sleeves and fix them. God bless America.

Now if you'll excuse me, I think I see a robin on the lawn.

Lilac Season

ONE OF THESE EVENINGS, the scent of lilacs is going to come drifting through the bedroom window. You'll be falling asleep and there it will be—that heady, almost cloying cachet that announces the end of early spring and the beginning of a warmer, loamier, more romantic period.

It's a small-town, midwestern phenomenon. A dreamy, once-a-year thing worthy of Rogers and Hammerstein. If there's an ounce of callow adolescent left in your jaded soul, the lilacs will find it and coax it out.

When the lilacs come out, it can be prom season—even for old folks. Lilac bushes are long-lived, and it's nice to think the same lilacs that are blooming tonight were blooming on those evenings when you were young and your hormones were raging, not sparking and sputtering the way they are now.

Careful, though. The scent of those lilacs can trigger lots of other deep-seated memories. No other blossom can go from "romantic spring evening" to "drugstore perfume counter" or, worse yet, "aging grandma" in a single whiff.

Then there are the lilac flowers themselves—tall bunches of them clipped from bushes and arranged in tall vases on kitchen tables or living room pianos or bedroom dressers. Lilacs are peasant flowers and prefer ordinary vases—Woolworth vases or even tall plastic pitchers. Your basic lilac bunch doesn't respond well to crystal.

For Catholics of a certain age, lilacs invoke memories of May as Mary's month. Back then, every girl was named Mary Something: Mary Beth, Mary Pat, Mary Ruth, Mary Jo, Mary This, Mary That. Year in, year out, Mary Whoever got to lead the school procession. And every classroom statue and shrine to the Virgin was festooned with bunches and bunches of lilacs.

For people who grew up on farms, lilacs invoke memories of home and the lilac bush outside the mudroom door or the hedge halfway across the yard on the way to the barn.

For flower lovers, lilacs are the promise of perennial pleasures to come. If we have lilacs, can peonies and hydrangeas and clematis be far behind?

It will all start any night now with the faintest hint of a scent from a bush out there somewhere. Hot darn. Put on an extra blanket. Throw the bedroom window open a little wider. Get ready to feel starry-eyed and vaguely discontented. The lilacs are coming, and it may as well be spring.

Meditation on a Green Minivan

SOCRATES said the unexamined life is not worth living. Amen, brother. I couldn't agree more. I examine my life all the time. I contemplate my flaws, note my sins and transgressions, and work hard to balance the karmic books.

In examining my life, I think I may have hit on the central question—the one that, if answered, will solve the riddle of my existence and make everything absolutely clear in perpetuity.

Why am I always stuck behind green minivans on the freeway?

Other drivers move in and out of traffic. Openings appear for them. A blink of the turn signal and they are on their way, simple smiles on their vacant faces. No doubt they are listening to "lite" rock with less talk and fewer interruptions.

I am pinned in the right lane, a rusty Camry in my blind spot, a green minivan directly in front of me.

In my younger days, I worked my way out of situations like these with a combination of horn, accelerator, and middle finger. Now that I have had time to examine my life, I see that I was wrong. Rage was not the answer. I was swimming against the current. For every green minivan I flipped off, two green minivans rolled off an assembly line somewhere and onto the freeway ahead of me.

Better to proceed at the speed of the green minivan ahead of me (usually five miles an hour slower than I personally would prefer to go). Better to remain calm and contemplate small details on the tailgate—the uninspired design of the lights, the bumper sticker advertising a child's honor student status, the smeary arc of the worn wiper blade on the rear window. Better to drive with a tranquil, empty mind.

Sometimes I use inane minivan model names, obviously focus group approved, for mantras: "oohhm . . . Windstar . . . oohhm . . . Town and Country."

They say there is room for seven passengers in there. They say there are storage compartments for everything. I say every green minivan comes with a spiritual lesson stowed in a special compartment just for me. It's standard equipment.

But what's the lesson? Why does fate always stick me behind green minivans on the freeway? What am I supposed to take away? Patience? Humility? Compassion? Wisdom? What?

The answer eludes me as surely as green minivans impede me, and I continue to examine life, trying to tease the truth out.

"Oohhm . . . Windstar . . . Oohhm . . . Town and Country."

I will finish this commentary, forward it to Minnesota Public Radio, and if they like it, I will hurry over to the studio to record it. I will take the freeway, and as I merge into traffic, there it will be. A green minivan. Right ahead of me, going five miles an hour slower than I want to go, dragging the meaning of life like a broken tail pipe.

They're Back

A FRIEND OF MINE up on the Cuyuna Range has established what I consider to be the O'Hare Airport of hummingbird feeders over the past few years. His hummingbirds are back from Mexico for another summer now, and the feeder is busy and crowded. There's an arrival or departure every few seconds from dawn until dark. If the space gets any more frenetic, the FAA will have to assign an air traffic controller.

If you just glance at the birds casually, they evoke a pleasant and fulfilling sense of natural harmony. Saint Francis of Assisi comes to you and whispers a prayer. But if you sit there and watch—really watch—a different picture emerges. Those hummingbirds are pushy little things. High-strung, grumpy, and selfish. North woods New Yorkers. To heck with Saint Francis. It's all about taking care of numero uno first.

They swoop in from a nearby white pine, hover, jostle one another until someone leaves, then tussle to take the departed bird's place. There's a high-metabolism urgency to it—"c'mon, c'mon, c'mon." It's like a crowded lunch hour sandwich counter. These birds could really use a tiny take-a-number system.

"Last evening there were so many I saw two drinking from the same port," my friend reports. "One sat on the perch. The other hovered just over its shoulder. They were both sucking sugar at the same time."

Such sharing is rare. At the feeder, it's all about "me first," and some birds are grumpier and pushier than others. They cut in front of whoever is waiting with an almost human "what are you going to do about it?" attitude. They're like single drivers bypassing the line at the ramp meter and using the high-occupancy vehicle lane.

And so it goes, sunrise to sunset. Quick three- and four-inch darting flights. Buzz-buzz-jostle-nudge, "Get out of my space." All in the service of self.

"I gotta be first. All the time," baseball legend Ty Cobb explained after beating a teammate to within an inch of his life over who had the right to the first shower after a game. The mighty Cobb and many other tormented egomaniacs seem to have returned, reincarnated as one-ounce balls of frantic, feathered furtiveness circling my friend's feeder—like news helicopters hovering over a big event.

At night, you get the idea that they're out there, perched in the dark, listening to their little hummingbird stomachs growl, struggling to slow their metabolisms down in order to make it to dawn and get back to feeding.

If there's a lesson to be learned in all this, maybe it's that we humans aren't the only species capable of selfishness. But we may be the only species capable of overcoming that selfishness and showing the world a bit of compassion. Maybe that's what we ought to do. Maybe the hummingbirds should teach us to be more kind and tolerant and generous to one another. What do you say? Let's give it a try.

You first.

What's the Rush?

IS IT JUST ME or are liberal arts schools around here scheduling graduation a little earlier every year? Inching it ahead on the calendar, shortening the semester, saving money even as they increase tuition. Handing the young people their diplomas, telling them, "So long. Stay in touch. Don't let the doors on Old Main hit you in the fanny on the way out."

What a rook. The kids miss out on those last precious late May weeks—sunbathing, Frisbee on the lawn, and those late senior year last-chance-before-graduation affairs of the heart, not to mention all those affairs of the keg.

Here in Minnesota, late May is one of the few times in the school year when the campus actually looks like it did in the recruitment brochure you saw in the high school guidance office—the brochure that got you interested in the school in the first place.

There's fall and the beautiful colors, and there's late May. The rest of the school year is like January in Moscow. Hundred-year-old radiators clank. The dorms smell like methane and the work-study janitor's sweeping compound. The food service smells like cabbage and the industrial dishwashing machine. Everyone has an academic postnasal drip. Crumpled, used-looking tissues litter quad hallway floors. Then late May arrives and the sunlight and open windows make everything right again.

Look, maybe these early graduation ceremonies would be all right if there were a real job market out there—if you shook the dean's hand and walked off the stage into a position with a living wage and a future and benefits. But no. In this economy, chances are you're moving back into your parents' basement—or as one of my kids' friends calls it, "Apartment 2B." The same kid calls his parents "the roommates."

Face it. The Class of 2009 is in for what Donald Rumsfeld called "a long, hard slog." The least the liberal arts schools could do is give them a couple more weeks on campus before reality sets in.

C'mon. Move graduation back where it belongs. It won't hurt anything. You'll be keeping new graduates off hide-a-beds in basements all over the country. Maybe even a hide-a-bed in a certain basement near me.

A Tiny Discrepancy

ONCE AGAIN THIS MOTHER'S DAY, my wife got love, adoration, pampering, a day of family togetherness, a gift certificate for a really good, really professional massage, and a dinner prepared by her kids—all of them good cooks. Once again this Father's Day, I will get a three-pack of tube socks from Target.

I'm not complaining, mind you. I'm not looking to scare up any trouble. No...unh-unh...mustn't go there...heaven forbid.

This Mother's Day–Father's Day inequity is simply the natural order of things—not just at our house—across the country. Mom gets good stuff—stuff from the heart. The Old Man gets a quick, cheap, practical after-thought. Clearly, the rules and routines for Mother's and Father's Days were developed by women for women. They drip with estrogen.

On Mother's Day when the kids were younger, for example, she wanted me to take them somewhere for the day so she could have a break. Then, when Father's Day came along, she thought it would be a good idea for me to take the kids somewhere for the day. It was a chance for me to spend some quality time with them.

To be honest, we fathers bring much of this down on ourselves. We don't wait for special days or gifts. We buy what we want when we want it—power tools, sporting goods, electronics, books—to heck with the family budget. Every day is Father's Day. Women and children understand this and factor it in.

Then there is the way we fathers behave when someone actually does give us something. We just don't trust gifts—or our own emotions when we get gifts. Gifts confuse and cow us. We grunt a half-hearted thank-you and adjourn to the couch to study the new object and think about how we should feel.

Mothers embrace Mother's Day. Fathers keep Father's Day at arm's length and take the fun out of it for the whole family in the process. I know a guy whose seven-year-old was just dying to tell him what the family had gotten him for Father's Day.

"I'll tell ya, Pop," the kid offered again and again. "If you wanna know, I'll tell ya."

The guy kept saying no. That it would ruin the surprise for the rest of the family.

The kid finally paused and thought it through.

"Okay," he said after a while. "I won't tell ya. But here's a hint: when you push a button the garage door goes up and down."

Children grow up. The exuberance fades. The family assumes a fundamentally matriarchal structure. Like old rogue bulls off in the brush at the edge of the elephant herd, fathers exist at the periphery.

The periphery. To which, unwrapped tube socks in hand, I will return from my moment in the Father's Day limelight just as quickly as possible this Sunday, muttering, "Tube socks. Just what I needed. Yessir, how 'bout that? New tube socks."

Is Ambivalence the Perfect Father's Day Gift?

SOMETHING THERE IS THAT does not love Father's Day. The whole thing feels so left-handed and lumpy and self-conscious somehow. Truth be told, most fathers would just as soon skip Father's Day and have a regular old summer Sunday instead.

It's the pressure of being the center of attention. Every other day of the year, we sit there and listen as our wives and children talk about us as if we weren't even in the room—as if we were Labrador puppies they were trying to paper train. We're used to being overlooked, underestimated, and unappreciated. We like it.

Then along comes Father's Day and we're expected to be gracious and accept all the attention, and we're not good at it. Feigning gratitude for all the gifts we didn't want, for example. Cheap screwdriver and socket sets that end up in the kitchen junk drawer. Manicure kits made in China. Nose hair trimmers. Polo shirts. Socks.

Gosh, thanks. No, really, thanks. They're just what we always wanted. We just didn't know we wanted them.

Fathers are notoriously bad at receiving gifts because we're guys. As guys we pretty much buy whatever we want whenever we want it. No budget constraints. No saving up for it. I have an uncle, the father of eleven, who stopped at a bar on the way home from work. The bar was for sale. He bought it on the spot. I have a brother, the father of two, who bought a seven-thousand-dollar bicycle the same way.

Where do you think all those power tools come from? And those sports cars, video game systems, and flat-screen TVs?

When you're a guy, every day is Father's Day as long as you lay low and don't call attention to yourself.

So if you're looking for the perfect Father's Day gift for someone special this year, why not give him what he really wants? Give him the gift of ambivalent apathy—the same ambivalent apathy you give him the rest of the year. Put a big stack of pancakes in him. Then let him lump up on the couch with the remote control. It's normal, and he loves normal. It's a celebration of his real place in the family.

And isn't that what Father's Day is all about?

Tacky, Tacky, Tacky

SPRING HAS SHUFFLED OFF THE STAGE. Summer is all but officially here. Up and down the block, the neighbors are out in force, weeding, fertilizing, hanging baskets of begonias, plugging planters with pansies, frantically troweling annuals into the earth. Their perennials are beginning to stir, too. In flowerbed after flowerbed, lilies, peonies, roses, and hydrangeas are waking up and getting ready to go to work.

Minnesotans put a lot of time and thought into their lawns and gardens this time of year. They are, after all, Minnesotans. Times are tough though, and personally, I have line-item vetoed further lawn- and garden-related expenditures. This year we will once again go with our cheap, quick, easy, classically Minnesotan motif.

I refer, of course, to dandelions and creeping charlie. As I write this, our yard is a riot of yellow flowers going to seed. Here and there, pockets of purple creeping charlie provide a subtle counterpoint. The effect is striking, although whether it says "carefree homeowner" or "there goes the neighborhood" depends on whether or not you're one of those keep-up-with-the-Joneses types.

We stopped trying to keep up years ago. The Joneses weren't just way ahead when we quit. They'd lapped us. Several times. It looks like they'll lap us again this year with their new plantings and fertilizers and weed killers and automatic sprinkler systems. Darn those Joneses anyhow.

I've never trusted those weed-and-feed products. And I don't like those fertilizers you spray on with the hose. The only fertilizers on our lawn come factory direct—from neighborhood dogs. The greens they produce are remarkable, if somewhat patchy.

Unlike the Joneses, we don't tear everything out and start new whenever tastes change. This is Minnesota, gosh darn it. Planting a perennial is a commitment. Once it's in the earth, you're in for the long haul. It's till death do you part, not till something trendier comes along.

Who knows what kind of statement the Joneses are trying to make with that patch of blue tufted prairie grass over by the fence. The patch of lilies by the front walk in our yard came from my wife's Grandma Selma's flowerbed on the farm. The statement they make says "sturdy" and "self-reliant." And if those orange flowers clash with the yellow of our dandelions and the purple of our creeping charlie, the Joneses don't have to worry. By mid-August the entire yard will take on a hue I like to think of as a rich, sun-bronzed brown.

People Watching at Lake Calhoun

I LOVE TO PEOPLE WATCH. Especially here in Minnesota. There's a bench by the sidewalk on the east side of Lake Calhoun that's perfectly positioned to do just that. It's a front-row seat for the human parade, a perch unlike any other. If you're a writer, it's an all-but-required form of observation. Here are the subjects of your stories. Here is a procession unto itself. Hour after hour, day after day, Calhoun produces a steady stream of stalwart little sagas, scenes, conversations, and people.

Young people. Old people. Lovers and friends. Promenaders. Power walkers. Joggers. Toddlers peeping back at you from strollers. Dogs and dog owners of all shapes and sizes. The beautiful. The damned. The eccentric. People lost in thought. People who don't appear to have strung two synapses together—ever.

This is Minnesota, and there is no shortage of great places to sit and people watch. We have our downtown lunch hour parks and skyways, our malls, our theater lobbies at intermission, and the State Fair, of course. But day in and day out, Lake Calhoun is Minnesota's best people-watching venue, hands down. We're more comfortable with ourselves there—more at home. When a friend calls and suggests a walk around Calhoun, we come as we are. We'd make the trek in our walking shoes and bathrobes if the park police would let us.

And now that summer has returned, I can report that winter did nothing to diminish Minnesota's inventory of paint-spattered sweatpants and comfortable old t-shirts promoting every rock band, every corporation, college, and nonprofit organization on the planet—and t-shirts featuring every quirky little pun and advocating every side of every cause in human history. Those beer-bellied guys who strip off their t-shirts and stroll around Calhoun topless have made it through the dark months, too.

Sit on that bench long enough and you will see just about everyone and everything the state has to offer. Sit quietly enough and you will realize this is a great, good place—and has been for a long time.

With the economy in the tank, you can't beat the price of admission. It's free. One hundred percent free. Seating is limited, though. So if you get to the bench before I do, save me a spot. Feel free to start people watching without me.

Little League. Big Problem.

LITTLE LEAGUE BASEBALL SEASON is upon us again —that time of year when parents take a fun-to-play game, suck every last ounce of spontaneity out of it, and smother whatever is left with teachable moments, character building, and overorganization.

Kids don't sign up for Little League. Kids don't even like baseball anymore. Can you blame them? Honestly now—would you sign up for Little League if you had a PlayStation?

It's all those parents out to compete with other parents. They're the ones. They are why family weeknights orbit around practice for seven-, eight-, and nine-year-olds. They are why the family schedule is cratered with games every weekend.

Luckily, thanks to a perverse form of parental karma, parents have to pay big time. They not only have to coach, they have to groom diamonds before games, staff snack stands during games, and pick up litter afterward, too.

Most onerous of all, they have to sit through inning after mind-numbing inning where no one gets a hit, everyone either gets hit by a pitch or draws a walk, and the teams change sides because so many runners have scored, not because the team at bat made three outs.

Then there is the inevitable trip down to a major league game with the rest of the parents and all those kids. The tickets seem reasonably priced, but there's the parking, the food, and the souvenirs. You can't get yourself and a kid in and out of the stadium for much less than forty dollars. And chances are you're going to wind up taking all your kids to the game, not just the ballplayer. Get ready to kiss a C-note good-bye.

Trust me on this. I've had four kids play Little League. I know. It wasn't until late in the game that I figured a way out of it.

Want to avoid the hassle? Here's what you do: Whenever the kid mentions Little League, turn away from the television, look down the couch, and hand the child the remote control. Then say, "Let's watch what you want to watch for a while." One hour of tedious kid TV trumps a summer of peer-pressured parents every time.

Thanks, Mom

I JOINED FACEBOOK last week, in spite of myself. I find social networking as unnerving as a drunken office party. Still, you have to stay in touch. So I signed up, and almost immediately, Facebook suggested I link to a guy I hadn't seen in more than a quarter century. He grew up across the street, the only son of a germophobic mother. Sitting there, staring at the middle-aged face of the kid from across the street, I remembered an incident involving his mother and his baseball glove.

Back then, your glove and how you broke it in said a lot about you. It was how you rolled it. You oiled it. You pounded a ball into the pocket hour after hour, and you worked at getting the glove to hinge closed just right. It was the endless pursuit of perfection.

He had the same glove I did, a three-fingered fielder's glove from the Sears, Roebuck catalog—a quintessentially versatile model. If you broke it in right, you could play any position with it—outfield, infield, even first base or catcher in a pinch. Mine was better, primarily because I played more baseball with it. His was more of a prop, an accessory to his kidhood. It wasn't as supple. It didn't flop shut around hot line drives.

Then came that terrible morning when he came out to play and showed us his freshly laundered, still soggy mitt.

"She washed it," he said. There were tears in his eyes. "She actually put it in the washing machine and washed it."

A day or two later, his glove sprouted mold. Mold meant germs, and a day or two after that, his mother threw it away. He never replaced it. Adolescence was looming and he wasn't really a ballplayer.

High school came. Then college. We lost touch. Then, suddenly, there he was on Facebook. Highly successful, influential, confident. But I could see that slight chink in his psyche. That hidden vulnerability. That Achilles' heel. After a while I closed Facebook and e-mailed my own mother.

"Dear Mom," I began, "Thanks for not washing my baseball glove . . ."

Meditation on a Lawnmower

A SAMURAI GETS A SWORD. A Minnesotan gets a mower. A twenty-inch power lawnmower. It is yours. You journey through life with it. More than a simple tool, your mower has a spirit of its own. It's a link to your agrarian roots and small-town past.

The engine, for example. It's a simple, foolproof, timeless design. Your great-great-uncle Emil would recognize it and be able to tune it up immediately, were he to come back.

There is contemplative perfection in your mower's narrow twenty-inch deck, too. Sure, a narrow deck means more work. And sure, you could go to one of those superstores and buy a flashier mower that cuts wider and also mulches—or worse yet, a ride-on model. But you'd just get done faster and upstage the neighbors. So stick with your properly Minnesotan twenty-inch deck. It was good enough for your father and his father before him. It's good enough for you.

Besides, your inner Minnesota contemplative knows there is virtue in mowing slowly. It's a chance to meditate, to take emotional inventory. So go ahead, mow slow. Contemplate the sins of your past life as you push. Heck—work out the meaning of life itself. Find your place in the infinite space-time continuum.

Or sing to yourself. Your mower will understand. Just try not to let the words get stuck crossways in your brain where they can repeat themselves over and over and drive you mow-crazy.

There are so many little lessons to learn in mowing. So many opportunities to become a better person. Say, for example, you mowed over your seven iron, left out in the grass and the rain for days by your eleven-year-old.

Is it the child's fault for simply being a child? Your fault for fertilizing the lawn too zealously (thus having the grass grow too quickly and hide the club)? Or is it an opportunity to replace the seven iron with some newer, more high-tech club? Your inner contemplative will know.

The years will pass. You and your mower will grow old together. In time, you will both start to sputter and run rough. There will be trips to the doctor and the small-engine repair shop, but the time will come when you and your mower will part ways for eternity.

And as you lay there, at peace, having fought the good fight to be the best Minnesotan you could possibly be, your inner contemplative will sense the grass close by, still growing, and you will smile a wise, all-knowing smile. Because you will know that every Tuesday morning, rain or shine, they send a crew out to the cemetery to mow.

A Minnesota Must

JUNE should be Boat Ride in Minnesota Month. Everyone in the state ought to be required by law to go spend an afternoon in a boat on a quiet little lake under a cool, high, perfectly blue Minnesota sky. Not some big power-boat or some pontoon. A rowboat, with real oars and oar-locks that squeak as you pull your way across the water. And an anchor made from a coffee can full of concrete tied to the boat with fifteen feet of nylon rope.

Lay back in the bow. Use a boat cushion for a back-rest and close your eyes. Let a dragonfly buzz by. Listen to the little waves lap at the boat. Indulge in this time-honored form of Minnesota meditation. The swamis of the East have their lotuses; we have our lily pads. Instead of saying "ohhm," try muttering "uff-da—hot enough for ya?" to whoever it is you're sharing your boat ride with.

Don't feel obligated to fish. Good lord, no. I mean, you can if you want to. But you can bring a good book along—a summer book that will let you idle the hours away without having to think too hard. One of my favor-ite Junes of all time was the June my Aunt Dorothy spent reading Raymond Chandler paperbacks while Uncle Roger flailed away with his bait-casting rig in search of a big fish on the delightfully misnamed Musky Bay.

There's a sense of proportion to an afternoon in a rowboat. A perspective you won't experience in a run-about or a bass boat or a ski boat racing across the water with kids on a tube in tow. A rowboat can transport you back to the days when cabins really were cabins, not lake homes with big lawns and intricate docks and fancy electric boat lifts.

One rowboat ride a year for every man, woman, and child in Minnesota, preferably a June rowboat ride. With ten thousand lakes and hundreds of thousands of rowboats, we'd be doing the whole state a great contemplative good.

On Finding a Bungee Cord

I'm out bicycling the other day. I come around a corner and find a perfectly good bungee cord on the road. I stop. I pick it up, and just a little happier somehow, I take it with me.

"All right," I think. "A free bungee cord. Right there in the road."

How very fortunate. How very Minnesotan. I don't know how they look on finds like this elsewhere, but around here, finding a perfectly good bungee cord on the road ranks right up there with finding a four-leaf clover or having a five-dollar bill come blowing down the sidewalk. A found bungee cord is a tether that stretches from you back to whoever lost it. It's an omen. It's spiritual connective tissue that flew out of someone else's life directly into your path. It's a cautionary tale that Fate tells you for a reason.

Contemplate your new bungee cord. Where was it going? What was it holding down when it left its former owner and came to you? The trunk of a '78 Monte Carlo?

A canoe on car tops headed for the Boundary Waters? A bike rack? A tarp? A trailer tailgate?

We Minnesotans are collectors at heart. Everybody holds onto something—salt and pepper sets, pennies, gum wrapper foil, something. An old neighbor of mine who worked at the airport for forty years had a drum full of lost luggage tags in his garage. I once met a guy over near Brainerd who was an estate sale junkie and had snapped up more than fifty pairs of vise grips.

No doubt about it. Minnesotans are collectors. Think we aren't? Then answer me this: is Minnesota not home to the world's largest ball of twine?

My latest roadside bungee has joined all the others on a peg out in the garage. I'm not sure what I'm supposed to do with it yet, but Fate will send me some purpose. Some kid will be moving out. Or a neighbor will have some huge box in the trunk of his car.

"Just a minute," I'll say.

I'll go to the garage and come back with the bungee cord. "You really ought to tie that down."

And whoever it is will thank me and say they'll bring it back.

"Nah," I'll say. "Keep it. I find 'em on the road all the time."

In Praise of Municipal Golf

MINNESOTA may be up to here in new, hundred-and-ten-dollar-a-round golf courses, but give me a twenty-buck municipal nine-holer every time. The kind of course that a bunch of local guys got together and punched in after World War II. The kind they call "the country club," in spite of the fact that it doesn't have a pool or a dress code or dances. In spite of the fact that anyone who shows up can play.

While the corporations that built the new courses turned to millionaire golf architects to lay out every hole to fit the land perfectly, the guys who built the municipal course just kind of figured Number Three ought to go where it did. Some of the most memorable and eccentric holes in Minnesota golf happened that way.

Like the right-angle par four dogleg up in Stearns County where you could cut the angle and go for the green if you just had the nerve to aim over the seniors sunning themselves on the patio at the nursing home. Or the par three across the water hazard up in Walker where a young black bear hung out all summer a few years ago.

Right here in the Twin Cities, we have Fort Snelling Golf Course—nine holes shorter and more eccentric than your great-aunt Dorothy, the whole track gerrymandered into a tiny piece of the old Fort Snelling parade ground.

It's all right angles and aggravatingly small greens. Every couple of minutes, the bucolic setting echoes with the roar of arriving and departing jet traffic at the airport next door.

There are no bent grass fairways at Fort Snelling, just regular old municipal park grass. The last time I played it, the dandelions had gone to seed—Fort Snelling's answer to the azaleas at Augusta National, where they play the Masters every spring.

Let those new courses scramble to establish some sort of hallowed golfing tradition. We've got all the tradition we need. It's a half mile out of town "on the tar road." You can't miss it. Those municipal courses were good enough for generations of Minnesota golfers. They're good enough for me.

I was golfing at one of them with a buddy one day. We were teeing up on a par three when he suddenly remembered: this was the hole where his devoutly Catholic father-in-law had gotten a hole in one. His father-in-law had gone now—passed on. So we bowed our heads and remembered the man a little. Then it was time to hit away.

"Doc," my buddy said, waggling his club, "If you're up there, give us some kind of sign." And just like that, the bells on the local Catholic church rang the Angelus.

Go ahead and pay a hundred and ten bucks a round if you want. But a hundred and ten bucks won't ever get you service like that.

Who Turned on the Air Conditioning?

My children are Norwegian on their mother's side. As soon as the temperature hits eighty degrees, they close up the house, run to the thermostat, and turn on the air conditioning.

As father, resident non-Norwegian, curmudgeon, and miser, I protest. Bitterly. Don't they know how much air conditioning costs? Aren't they ashamed to be hot weather wimps? I huff, mutter, bluster, and scowl—and turn the air conditioning off. But I am outnumbered. And outsmarted. They wait until my back is turned and switch the air conditioning on again. This time of year I live in a three-bedroom Frigidaire. It may be ninety out there, but in here we're wearing sweatshirts and huddling under blankets.

The huge compressor on the north side of the house whirrs and clanks in the neighbor's direction. I would feel guilty about the noise if the same neighbors weren't running their air conditioner, whirring and clanking back at us. It's the same with the neighbors on the other side. When the temperature hits ninety, every house on the block gets sealed up tight. Every compressor whirrs and clanks. Our tranquil, tree-lined street sounds like a truck stop parking lot while we sit inside in cold, morgue-like solitude.

What happened, Minnesota? When it got hot in the old days, people accepted it. They opened the windows and sweltered. At night, they hauled bedding outside and slept fitfully under the stars with the mosquitoes and heat lightning flashing somewhere out there over the Dakotas.

Somewhere, generations of my children's Norwegian ancestors are looking on, shaking their heads. They were some tough old coots back in their day. This new generation has gone pretty darned soft, in spite of that non-Norske father of theirs.

And the old ones are right. It's a pretty sad day when that old Norwegian Minnesotan expression "hot enough for ya?" becomes "hot enough for air conditioning yet?"

Homegrown Tomatoes

HANG AROUND MINNESOTA LONG ENOUGH and you start to divide each season into miniseasons—into events you use to mark the passing of the season and reassure yourself the world has not gone completely nuts. In that spirit, I'm happy to announce Minnesota is about to embark on the happiest miniseason of summer—Homegrown Tomato Season.

All over the state, backyard tomato vines—vines that began life in egg carton planters on south-facing kitchen windowsills last February—are about to deliver the first tomatoes of the season. Thousands of tomato-loving Minnesotans are about to pick that first sun-warmed, vine-ripened tomato, hurry to the kitchen, grab the saltshaker, and go for it.

Nothing is as wholesomely hedonistic. Standing there, awash in the scent of fresh-picked tomato, juice dribbling down your chin, you feel like you must have committed some cardinal sin—possibly several.

And in Minnesota, the backyard tomatoes come in with a vengeance. No other garden plant goes from 0 to

160 quite like a Minnesota tomato vine during a July hot spell. These things don't just ripen. They riot. Suddenly, the whole state is up to here in tomatoes.

You know it's Homegrown Tomato Season when grocery bags full of free tomatoes appear on the counter near the coffeepot at work. We've got lumber and grain exchanges. This time of year, Minnesota needs a tomato exchange—a place where backyard tomato growers can trade extras with other growers—an "I'll take yours if you take mine" kind of thing.

Homegrown Tomato Season lasts until first frost or you've had your fill and lose interest—whichever comes first. You know it's over when you look down and see some big old bubba of an overly ripe tomato, still attached to the vine, lying, split open, on the ground.

You'll feel guilty about it, but it's a good guilty somehow. There's a time to every purpose. Homegrown Tomato Season will be over, not to be thought of again until the seed catalogs arrive next winter.

For now though, it's Homegrown Tomato Season all across Minnesota. Bring on the tomatoes and pass the saltshaker. Life is sweet.

Still Going Out for the Team

THE DAYS ARE HOT. The nights are cool. The sun, riding just a bit lower in the sky, produces a beautiful yellow-tinged light. It's two-a-day football practice season in Minnesota, and something deep in the soul of every old high school football player yearns to suit up and lope out onto the practice field once more.

They are organized, methodical training sessions these days, but two-a-days used to be a much simpler rite of passage. They were not just exercise. They were exercises in pain—and all the more basic aspects of coming-of-age male group activities. Coach called you "Melon Head," and there was a certain bouquet to the equipment he issued you—eau de old sweat. This was not new equipment. Putting your helmet on for the first time was like moving into one of those cheap, very lived-in apartments just off campus in college. It wasn't all that clean. You weren't sure what had happened in there, and you were glad you didn't know.

The workouts themselves didn't exactly appeal to the human spirit, but with a little experience—certainly by the time you were a junior—life on the verge of dehydration and heatstroke became oddly contemplative. You taught yourself to go to a more peaceful and serene place. You learned how to send yourself on a vision quest—pads, athletic supporter, and all.

Every year during two-a-days, our coach would make a ham-handed attempt to instill a sense of pride and tradition in the squad. He would have the old guy who had served as team trainer since the Roosevelt administration give a speech. The man would bring himself to tears remembering a glory that never was. Our school had a tradition of absolute mediocrity. Fifth place: that was our goal. Year in, year out, we would begin two-a-days hoping to finish in the middle of the conference. Year in, year out, we would end the season having failed to achieve even that. Looking back, I now see the man was crying tears of futility. Two-a-days had barely started, but he knew we were going to give him yet another season about which to cry.

All that said, it's still two-a-day season. The voice of the old high school football player deep within me says, "Let's get out there. Let's go." Luckily, another, more geezerly voice usually pipes up about then: "Stick a fork in it, Melon Head. You're done."

Start the State Fair without Me

YOU REACH A POINT in a day at the State Fair when your senses kick into overdrive and everything comes rushing at you like one of those surreal "our hero is going crazy now" montages in a Hitchcock film. For me, that point is about fifteen feet inside the front gate.

There's the crowd, to begin with—the way it mills and churns and wanders aimlessly. There's always someone in front of you, always someone coming at you. Young people. Old people. Toddlers on leashes. All of them vacant eyed, shuffling along, as if they were on psychotropic medication in a big, outdoor locked ward. The only ones who don't appear to be overmedicated are the young and hormonal, but they don't seem to be able to walk without desperately holding onto one another and pausing to demonstrate their affection every few feet.

There is the noise. The carnival rides roaring past. People screaming. The "yowsa-yowsa" of the barkers. Oompah bands. Barbershop quartets. High school marching bands. TV stations. Hip-hop radio stations.

And the sound from whatever is going on at the grandstand spilling out over absolutely everything.

There are cheap gizmos and whatchamacallits for sale—devices designed to solve problems and alleviate conditions on the more depressing periphery of life. Carbuncle creams. Wrinkle steamers. Knee and back braces. That kind of stuff.

There's that oily patina your skin acquires as you lurch, addle-brained, past all those deep fryers. Suddenly you, too, are emitting that State Fair smell—part cotton candy and part corn dog with a hint of lunch counter and farm animal manure—from every pore.

On the positive side, you can't beat the people watching. It's just that the whole time you're watching people, people will probably be watching you. Sitting on a curb near the carousel one year, I suddenly realized a five-year-old was observing me as if I were a great ape in a cage. I remember it vividly. He was studying me. His snow cone was melting over his knuckles. It was grape.

So with all due respect, no State Fair for me this year. Maybe next year. You go ahead. Have a great time. I'll just stay home and—you know—wash the car . . . mow the lawn . . . putter . . . all by myself . . .

A Fifties Flashback

I WENT FOR A WALK the other afternoon. I took my regular route through one of those post–World War II neighborhoods full of houses built for GI Bill couples. Houses that, like the first kids to grow up in them, are in their fifties now.

Everyone in America knows the look and the floor plan: two bedrooms, one bath, kitchen, and living room. Front door, kitchen door. Picture window. Maybe a brick fireplace in the upscale version. The original models came with an unfinished basement—a space that would eventually become the rumpus room. Most had detached one-car garages, although sometimes the garage was connected to the house by a narrow, screened breezeway.

Back when they were built, every house looked pretty much like the one next door. Today, each house has a look and personality of its own. Five decades of owners have added dormers or changed the roofline to make bedrooms out of attics. Some people have built additional rooms onto the back. Others have succumbed to suppertime telephone sales pitches and gone with aluminum siding.

The trees and the landscaping have matured, too. Today, any experienced homeowner can appreciate the foresight the original owners put into their plantings. But you can also spot the horticultural problems that come with time—a branch hanging over a roof here, an overgrown yew or rebellious hydrangea to be grubbed out there.

There is something positive and reassuring about neighborhoods like this. Young couples settled down and raised kids here, then sold to young couples who settled down and raised kids. Those couples eventually sold to young couples who settled down and raised kids, too. Now those couples are selling to young couples, some of whom I would surmise intend to settle down and raise kids.

This place has been kid-friendly from the start. Who knows how many metric tons of peanut butter and jelly sandwiches have been consumed here? Or how many gallons of milk for that matter. Listen closely and you can hear the echoes of half a century of screen doors slamming and five generations of mothers calling, "In or out—not both!"

Houses in neighborhoods like this are just the right size. They feel simple and honest and unpretentious. Keeping up with the Joneses is relatively easy and inexpensive. With a little luck, you can get by with a fresh coat of paint this year and maybe a new hardware store trellis for the clematis.

It's a new age, one that many of the people who originally owned these homes could never have dreamed possible. But it's also a fitful, nervous age. I can't help but wonder if maybe we all wouldn't sleep better in nice little two-bedroom homes with rumpus rooms in the basement and maybe a bike or two left out on the front lawn by kids in a hurry to get home for supper.

Acorns and Toyotas

COOL AUGUST NIGHT. Bedroom window open. Breeze in the old white oak out front. Drifting off to sleep. All is right with the world—except for the acorns letting go.

You can hear them succumbing to gravity a block away, carpet bombing the neighborhood, punctuating these late summer nights. They clack on the bedroom gable, rattle down the shingles, and plink off the gutter en route to the driveway below. They fall directly into the hosta bed or onto the lawn with a somewhat softer thud. I'll rake them up later. Either that or the neighborhood squirrels will harvest them and stash them away for winter.

Every so often, one of them ricochets off the neighbor's Corolla with a distinctive not-quite clunk, not-quite plink. Up in the bedroom, on the verge of sleep, I smirk a little. The neighbor's Corolla—heh, heh, heh. It's not nearly as amusing when they plunk my car.

So many acorns. Millions falling all over town, littering sidewalks and bike paths, crunching under car tires. They say Newton discovered gravity when a falling apple hit him on the head. I don't buy it. I say he was probably thumped by an acorn. Only last Saturday, a guy I was golfing with got plunked good and hard as he teed up his ball in a shady tee box.

The August acorn shower. Like the annual meteor shower, the first red sumac leaves, the State Fair, crickets in the night, or posters with the hometown high school football schedule showing up in store windows along Main Street, it's another little sign the season is changing.

Summer isn't over. Not quite yet. But the end is at hand. The bell is tolling loud and clear—loud and clear as an acorn clanking off the neighbor's Corolla.

The neighbor's Corolla—heh, heh, heh.

4 Sale

I SAW THE SADDEST LITTLE FIBERGLASS BOAT for sale the other day. It was in the weeds in the ditch at the side of the road. Somebody had spray painted the number "4" and the word "Sale" on a weathered piece of plywood and propped it up against the boat's trailer. The boat was maybe sixteen feet long and mustard yellow, and judging from the hull style and the tired old outboard clinging to its transom, I'd guess it was forty years old. It came from that era when the Baby Boom was young and single.

Flying by at 65 miles per hour, I could imagine two or three couples aboard, wearing swimsuits and dancing a frantic frug to a surfing song à la Frankie and Annette. It had been a lighthearted little boat in its day.

But then the Boomers had fallen in love and married and settled down and had kids and sold the boat to someone who used it for a few years. Then he'd sold it to someone who used it for fishing up at the cabin. Then he'd sold it—and so on and so forth. With every sale and every new owner the sad little boat got a little more tired and a little more worn out.

Here in the Land of 10,000 Lakes, we've all been aboard boats like this. The kind with screwdrivers and vise grips and spray cans full of strange hydrocarbon-based fluids underfoot. The kind that smells of gas and oil and mold. The kind that doesn't start the first time you turn the key. The kind where you instinctively check to make sure there's a paddle on board before you leave the dock.

Parked in that ditch, wearing that cruel "4 Sale" sign, the sad little boat had gone the way of all stuff. Its fiberglass had faded. Its trailer had rusted. God knows how many problems or leaks it might spring. It was autumn, too, hardly the peak of the used boat season.

I'll bet that in all of Minnesota, no one—absolutely no one—got up that morning and thought, "What a beautiful day. I think I'll buy a forty-year-old boat out of the ditch."

I looked at the boat in the rearview mirror. "There's an allegory in there somewhere," I thought. "Either that or a metaphor. Or a simile—or a parable. One of those literary things. Who knows what they call them anymore?"

A curve in the highway took the boat out of sight. "An allegory?" I thought. "A metaphor? What the heck is it?"

I turned the radio up and shrugged. Darned if I knew the term anymore. If I were twenty years younger, though, it would be right on the tip of my tongue.

Peter Smith is a veteran of Twin Cities advertising and a regular contributor to *Morning Edition* on Minnesota Public Radio. He writes magazine features, fiction, and occasional op-ed pieces for the *Star Tribune.* He and his wife live in Hopkins, Minnesota.